First Season

Felicity Amish

Copyright © 2024 by Felicity Amish

All rights reserved.

No portion of this book may be reproduced in any form without written permission from the publisher or author, except as permitted by U.S. copyright law.

Contents

Prologue	1
Chapter 1 - First Sight	2
Chapter 2 - Hooked	5
Chapter 3 - Cleo	10
Chapter 4 - Crush	14
Chapter 5 - Jealousy and a Red Dress	20
Chapter 6 - The Truth	26
Chapter 7 - A Chance	32
Chapter 8 - The Perfect Day	37
Chapter 9 - Bad News	44
Chapter 10 - A Promise	49
Chapter 11 - A Dare	55
Chapter 12 - Daniel	61
Chapter 13 - Bruises	67
Chapter 14 - The Nightmare Returns	74

Chapter 15 - Blaze	80
Chapter 16 - A Threat and a Mystery	88
Chapter 17 - Vandalism	96
Chapter 18 - Armour	103
Chapter 19 - Questions	111
Chapter 20 - Milkshakes and a Decision	121
Chapter 21 - Depth, Height, Speed	128
Chapter 22 - Sisters	136
Chapter 23 - Handcuffs and Consequences	144
Chapter 24 - Bad Memories	153
Chapter 25 - Someone To Talk To	163
Chapter 26 - Early Hope and Early Snow	170
Chapter 27 - A Miracle	179
Chapter 28 - A Fool For Love	188
Chapter 29 - New Beginnings	196
Chapter 30 - An Old Enemy and an Old Friend	203
Chapter 31 - Christmas	211
Chapter 32 - Not Enough Time	218
Chapter 33 - Snowstorm	227
Chapter 34 - Rescue	235
Chapter 35, Part 1 - Love Your Enemies	242
Chapter 35, Part 2 - December 31st	247
Chapter 36 - The Colour Red	251

Chapter 37 - Going Home   259

Epilogue   267

Prologue

EMMA

It was the first of September. The leaves had already begun to fall, and I had been feeling the same sorrow starting to grip me, the same way it always did at this time of year. Even though Stowe is breathtaking in the fall, I couldn't stop the sadness from creeping in. Bad memories had been coming back, and the nightmares with them. I had been fighting it, though. Smiling even when it made my face feel like a plastic mould, laughing even when I felt sick inside.

Things weren't looking good, let's just say. Then, today, I saw him. I'm not cliché, so I mean it when I say that there was something different about him. Something curious and wondrous cloaking his presence. I'm not normally poetic either, but I guess he brought that part of me out and into the light.

Bright blue eyes and auburn hair. Whatever it was about him, it drew me in.

Chapter 1 - First Sight

Before December 31st

AIDEN

"Hey, Aiden."

I had been lost in my thoughts, but my brain snaps to attention at the sound of a crystal clear, warm and flirtatious voice. It belongs to a girl with long legs, locks of strawberry blonde hair, rouge lips and perfect white skin. She winks at me as she walks past before I can reply, probably due to my jaw having dropped to the floor when I laid eyes on her.

As she walks away, I turn to Garth, who looks as star struck as I feel. He gazes down the hall at her as she leaves.

"Who is she?" I whisper.

"Only the most beautiful and wanted girl in the entire school. Emma Rayburn."

"Emma," I repeat. "How does she know my name?"

He shrugs nonchalantly. "She probably knows everyone's name. Girls are like that."

A slight smug smile tugs at my mouth. Emma knows my name. And Garth is jealous. "I think I'm in love."

"Oh no, buddy," Garth says, his tone mock sympathetic. "She may be drop dead gorgeous, but she is more famous for the fact that she hasn't dated anyone since sixth grade. And, hate to break it to you, but you don't stand a chance."

I punch him in the arm, hard. He laughs, rubbing the sore spot and shaking his head. "Says you," I scoff, but I'm smiling too.

Garth has a mop of unruly blond hair that is not always clean and a habit of laughing too loudly. He also loves to insult at my expense, but he's about the closest thing to a friend I have made in my first week at Stowe High School. Heck, he's my only proper friend in all of Stowe. He showed me around on my first day here and introduced me to his circle of friends that just happen to be weirdos, like him. But it's a new school and I'm a new kid, and I reckon I'm not doing too badly. Considering it's the second school I have ever been enrolled in.

"C'mon," he says. "Let's go eat."

At the cafeteria, we sit with Garth's group of friends. They complain about life, tease each other, tell the same stories they always tell and laugh. I laugh along now and then, but my thoughts are elsewhere. All through my funny-smelling-ham-and-wilted-lettuce-sandwich and my chocolate milk, I'm thinking about Emma. I wonder how a girl like her hasn't dated since sixth grade. And I wonder if there is any chance, even if it is minute, that I could change that.

~ ~ ~

EMMA

I walk into the school bathroom and take a shaky breath, half smiling when I remember the expression on his face. I can't remember the last time I was that bold.

I look in the mirror and bite my lip, sucking my stomach in and trying on a confident stance. I wonder how he sees me?

~ ~ ~

After December 31st

AIDEN

If I'm really honest, and I am honest these days, maybe I knew right from the start that it was the challenge I was attracted to. Challenges seem to have a habit of luring me in, even now. When I was eleven years old, my best friend, Mikayla, dared me to jump off the roof of her house. It was an irrational and really stupid dare, but because I couldn't turn away from a challenge, I accepted. I ended up with a broken leg and really ticked off parents. Mikayla, however, loved me after that. I don't know what it was, but she ended up having a crush on me right up until we moved away.

So maybe I couldn't resist the dare that I gave myself. Maybe I knew that, deep down. But sometimes, humans can know something and be completely oblivious of it at the same time. It's ridiculous, it's one of the thousands of reasons why life is so complicated, and it's true. Another thing that's for sure is that me being me, after my encounter with Emma and what Garth said about her, I would stop at nothing to make her mine.

Chapter 2 - Hooked

Before December 31st

AIDEN

My mom always says that I'm too curious. I think she means to say it's a flaw of mine, but in my own opinion, it can be beneficial. Knowledge is power, isn't it? And if I'm going to get Emma interested, I should at least know something about her past so that I can use it. Girls like boys to be resourceful, and sensitive to the things they deal with and have dealt with in their life. All of this makes sense to me as I mull it over in my mind and watch the clock on the wall of the classroom. School is almost over for the day, so my investigation will have to wait till tomorrow, since I'll need Garth's help.

Unless...

I haven't had Garth over to my house yet, but today is as good a day as any. I don't know of anyone else who can help me out and answer the few questions I have anyway.

When I get home, mom is cooking and dad is still at work. My mom is a writer, and she works from home. My dad is a paediatrician and more than once I've had the suspicion that he loves his job more than anything, even us. He's not bad, and I can say with a clear conscience that I love him, which is actually more than a lot of kids can say in the world today. I do love him. I just don't understand him.

"Hi, mom. Is it okay if a friend comes over for dinner?"

She raises an eyebrow. "Is it a girl?"

"Mom."

She smiles slyly. "Sure. As long as no homework is left undone."

I grab an apple and head upstairs. Inside my room, I chuck my backpack in a corner and sit down at my desk. I turn on my laptop and as soon as it's done starting up, I search Emma's full name on Facebook. Her profile picture is a full body shot of her and another girl with dark hair who is much shorter at a pool party. I study her appearance. I had already forgotten how stunning she was. I send her a friend request, take a bite of my apple and take my phone out of my pocket to text Garth.

He texts back that he'll be over in fifteen minutes.

I continue to scroll through her pictures. There's one where she's standing in front of a birthday cake, a smile on her face. I notice that somehow the smile doesn't reach her eyes, and that the same dark haired girl is next to her. In another picture, she's a-frame hugging a tall blond boy. I feel a small wave of jealousy pass over me right on cue. Or, at least, I think it's jealousy, even though I hardly know this girl.

There's a loud knock at my door that makes me jump. I close the tab on the computer and before I'm able to say 'Come in', my little sister bursts into the room.

I sigh at the sight of her, long red ringlets framing a face as mischievous as an imp. Stevie. She's nearly thirteen, full of nonsense, stubbornness, and occasionally, sweetness. Right now, I'm not feeling the sweetness vibe.

"What. Have I said. About bursting in." I growl.

She smiles a smile stickier than honey and prances over to me. "What are you doing?"

Her hand moves to the mouse to click on recently closed tabs, and I grab it. Did I mention she's also kind of nosy? "I think it's time for you to get out, freckles," I say, using the nickname I know she hates, as I snatch her other hand and pin both of her arms behind her back.

"Okay, okay!" she squeals and twists in my grip. "I just wanted to tell you that your weird friend is here."

I let go of her. "Couldn't you have told me that sooner?" She giggles and pirouettes out of the door.

I sigh and start downstairs to find Garth. He's waiting in the living room looking slightly awkward, while my mom hovers over him, spewing polite comments and questions in the voice she uses for new friends of mine.

"Mom..." I try to rescue Garth with a hidden hint in the tone of my voice.

"Oh Aiden, there you are, darling. I have some freshly baked cookies for you two. You are growing boys, after all." she smiles brightly, handing out a plate of heaped choc chip cookies to me, and I cringe a little.

"Thanks, mom." I take them from her and send an apologetic glance Garth's way. "We've got some...uh...homework to do, so we'll go now."

"Okay. Dinner is at seven, boys."

We get ourselves upstairs in a reasonably fast amount of time. Mom's enthusiasm is just her trying to be a good mom, but sometimes annoying.

Once inside my room again, I watch Garth take it in. It's pretty simple, honestly. A single bed in the corner, the walls painted dark grey, my hockey gear leaning against my desk and photo of my family on the desk next to my laptop are probably the most interesting features. It's usually kind of neat, since I can't take clutter. Unlike Stevie, whose pink room always ends up looking like a pink tornado again not long after she attempts to tidy it.

"Nice place," he says.

"Thanks." I stand back a little uncomfortably. I haven't brought anyone around since we moved, and I realize now that I was nervous about doing that.

"Your mom seems..." Garth begins, and I shoot him down with a look. I can't take it when people take jabs at my family, only I can do that. "Cool. She seems cool." he finishes safely.

I shrug. "Yeah, she is."

He glances at me in a funny way. "That's really all I was going to say. I mean it."

I relax a little. Huh, I think, this guy is more insightful than I thought. Which makes me glad that I have him a friend, and takes off a weight from my chest that I didn't know I was carrying. I guess I reckoned that the move would change a lot more things than it had, and knowing that it seemed I was going to be fine, that I was going to make friends and fit in, was a relief.

We munch cookies and chat about random, stupid things. I take my guitar out from under my bed and Garth reveals to me that he can play as well, and not half bad. After having a faux band rehearsal that ends in laughter because neither of us can sing, I bring up what's on my mind.

"So," I begin. "I have a plan."

"A plan?" Garth speaks through a mouthful of cookie.

"Yep. You remember we were talking about Emma Rayburn earlier?"

His expression turns cynical. Still chewing, he says, "Don't tell me you're thinking-"

"I am."

Chapter 3 - Cleo

Before December 31st

EMMA

I lie on my bed with my legs in the air. My sister is lying on the floor looking up at me as we talk.

I've considered telling her about Aiden quite a few times, but the sensible part of me dismissed the idea, knowing that she would be instantly concerned and watchful. I don't need that. It's taken forever for my family to learn that I don't want to be treated like a fragile flower, but they still do sometimes. It's not their fault, though. I know that if any of us could take back what happened that December night, we would, in a heartbeat. But we can't, so it looms over us, like a threatening raincloud.

"So. Patty." I say in a cheerful tone, shaking off the past. "What are you going to wear to Adrianne's party?"

"That forest green dress I have," she says, smiling up at me, her eyes dreamy. "and maybe pair it with my heeled pumps."

Dear Patty. I love my younger sister to bits. With her intelligent eyes that will no doubt look marvellous with that dress, her kind heart, and her lovable quirks. We are only eighteen months apart, and very close. I thank God for her all of the time, because sometimes I feel I wouldn't be able to do life without her. I also love Carpenter, my big brother, and Eddie, my little brother, but brothers are not the same as sisters.

"What about you?" she asks.

"I don't know if I'm coming, Pat." I look away for a moment and then back at her. I know she hates it when I refuse to leave the house, but she also understands that I am not always emotionally stable enough to do so.

"Emma! You have to. I don't want to go without you." She's frowning now, little creases between her brows.

"Oh, I just don't know if I'll enjoy it...but you must go."

She doesn't say anything for a while. I know what she's thinking, though. My mind wanders away as I listen to the rustle of leaves through the open window. First I'm thinking, how unfair that Patty looks so pretty when she's cross, because she's still frowning, meanwhile I look like a red tomato when I am angry. Then when I look outside the window again, I'm thinking how beautifully the leaves flutter to the ground as I watch them fall. And then, even though I don't want to think about him, I do. I think how I wouldn't mind going to the party if I knew he was going to be there.

~ ~ ~

AIDEN

Thursday. Midweek and all of the students at Stowe High School are just hanging in there till the weekend. Including me, and I only just started at this school.

I'm on my way to history class, daydreaming a little as I walk. Suddenly I crash into someone I didn't notice walking towards me, causing her to drop the books she was carrying. Classic, Aiden, classic. She's already hurriedly picking up her books when I crouch down to help her. I want to say sorry, but somehow it feels right for both of us to stay silent. She gives me one quick smile as I hand her the last book, 'A History of Modern Art', and is gone before I can ask her name, her wavy cocoa brown hair and shy demeanour leaving with her. Could've sworn I'd seen her somewhere before, but I can't remember where. I shrug to myself and stand up, finding that I'm only a few feet away from the classroom I was on my way to.

History would be okay, if the teacher was...well, not himself. Mr. Hardwell's surname suits him, being the plank of a man that he is. Hard on the outside and undoubtedly hard on the inside too. Tall, skinny, bespectacled and always smelling of smoke. One minute late to his class gets you in big trouble, and if my watch is correct, I'm already five minutes late.

I stand outside the door for a moment, definitely considering bunking, but because I've never bunked before anyways, I walk in.

I'm met by a full classroom of bored looking students and a fuming Mr. Hardwell.

"Mr. Harper!" he sputters, putting emphasis on the 'Mr'. "I'll thank you not to be late in the future again, ever, and to attend detention after school today."

Detention is way too big a punishment for being five minutes late, so I'm not afraid of that happening. "Sir, with all due respect, I'll do my best not to be late in the future. But, you and I both know I won't be in detention later today," I grin up at him with the cheesiest smile I have, and watch his face turn red. He's mostly bark and no bite, simply because he's not in a place high enough to carry out most of the threats he gives. The school would be a military school if he were to run it.

"You may sit, Harper. And I assure you, I have my eye on you." He hasn't liked me since I started here, and I have no idea why. But I can manage it.

Later, when I'm walking the school grounds to hockey practice, I find the girl I bumped into earlier. She's lying on her stomach atop the trimmed green grass, a pen in her hand and a drawing pad in front of her. She's concentrating so hard on whatever she's drawing that she doesn't notice me walking up.

"Hey," I say.

She startles, dropping her pen and snapping the pad shut. When she looks up at me, I notice she has dark, thick lashes. "Hi."

"What are you drawing that is so private?" I ask.

"Who are you that you think you should know?" she counters, calmly and not at all hostilely. But I see colour filling her cheeks.

I normally would have said bye and carried on to hockey practice, but something made me want to stay. I wanted to be friends with this girl.

"Nobody that should know. Just someone with enough curiosity to want to know." I sit down next to her. "You made me late for history class."

Half of her mouth turns up, in a charmingly crooked smile that makes her nose wrinkle. "You made me drop my books."

"Why were you carrying so many books anyway?"

She gets up to sit cross legged. "I love books."

"So do I, actually," I tell her. "I'm Aiden, by the way."

She holds out her hand. "Cleo."

Chapter 4 - Crush

A fter December 31st

AIDEN

I didn't see Cleo for at least a week and a half after that day when we first talked. Well, I saw her, here and there about the school, but somehow, perhaps because we were both busy or perhaps because we both had our minds on other things, we ended up ignoring each other. I regretted not asking for her number or something, but at the same time I just couldn't figure out where she'd fit into my life if I had. Every now and then, though, I'd remember her pretty eyes and my head would start spinning in a strange way...but I already had my heart set on Emma, and it wasn't too hard to think about her instead of Cleo. Well, that's what I told myself.

She really was a beautiful girl. Better looking by most guys' standards than Cleo in any case. I always tried to grab a place behind her in the waiting line in the cafeteria, and I'd watch her as she walked back to her table, her long body always elegant, her blonde hair almost always loose. She'd smile at me now and then, and whenever she did, I felt like I could fly.

But the smiles weren't satisfying enough. And when I heard about the party that everyone would be going to on Saturday, I figured it was about time I stop thinking and start acting.

I had to get myself invited to that party.

~ ~ ~

Before December 31st

EMMA

I wasn't sure if it was just in my head, but it seemed to me that Aiden was trying to get my attention. I had had plenty boys try it before, and I was used to playing it cold. But everything inside of me longs for my heart to finally be thawed. I'm scared, yes, but it has been a long time and that broken little twelve-year-old girl has turned into a five foot seven sixteen-year-old. And she is tired of playing it safe.

Another thing is that since I have 'met' Aiden, the nightmares have stopped. It's strange. For four years I've longed for them to stop, even prayed for them to stop, although I'm not as close to God as Patty and the rest of my family. I used to have this A3 poster on my wall with rainbow letters that said: Jesus is my hero.

But I took it down that December night.

I still go to church, and I haven't told my family that I don't consider myself a Christian anymore, but deep down I know I've made my decision.

Now the nightmares have finally come to a halt, long after I stopped praying or hoping they would.

And it coincides with meeting the boy named Aiden.

It's a Sunday afternoon and I'm sitting outside on the swing bench next to our pool, soaking up the weak sun. My friend, Crystalline, is sitting next to me. She prefers to go by Crystie so that most don't know her full name, which she has deemed ridiculous. I kind of like it, personally.

"Em? Did you not hear what I just said to you?"

Oops, I guess I zoned out while she was in the middle of saying something. "Um...wish I could say yes."

She rolls her eyes. "You've been doing this a lot lately, you know. You're not on something, are you?"

I shove her playfully. "Definitely. Got myself a dealer, want his number?"

She laughs her bubbly laugh. "Knew it. But wait, seriously, what's going on? Is it a guy?" And then her eyes grow round as she realizes what she just said.

I've asked her before not to go on about boys when she's with me, so no wonder she looks so concerned now. I have told her I want nothing to do with them and that I'm going to die an old spinster. She told me that if I am for real about that, she would join me and we'd live together and have lots of cats.

Crystie has been my friend for over three years now, and she's the only one who knows the dark secrets of my past, other than my family. She can be pushy and dramatic, but also the most loyal person I know. She sometimes doesn't think before she opens her mouth, but to me it just makes her more lovable.

"Didn't mean that." She quickly tries to change the subject. "You know, did I tell you, Bryan almost crashed our parents' car yesterday and-"

"Crystie! It's okay. I actually do want to talk to you about something like that."

Her eyes get even bigger. "Really?"

I nod. "But you have to promise not to tell anyone. Not Patty, or my brothers, or my parents. Or anyone else."

"I won't." She sticks her pinkie finger out and I hook it with my own. We've been doing this since age thirteen.

"There is a boy..."

"Oh Emma!" she squeals, "Wow!"

"Slow down! Slow down. I think I like him, but you have to understand that I don't even know him yet. Have you seen the new boy around at school? His name is Aiden."

She frowns as she thinks. "The one with the reddish hair?"

"Yeah."

"Hmm...interesting choice. He isn't classically good looking but he is like really tall, maybe six foot, and he has those eyes and his voice is kind of nice and-"

I cut her off again. "Seems like you've been observing him very closely."

"No, no, it's not like that, Em! I just...notice boys...a lot more than you think I do."

I feel kind of bad. I actually do know that she notices boys, it's just that I haven't given her any space to talk about it because I normally switch off when she even tries to start. She accepts it though and deals with it without complaining, but I know I haven't been a very good friend or listener. That's got to change. I want to turn over a new leaf, and be a little freer.

"Hey, I'm not mad at all. But this guy, I feel like he's...I don't know. Special? Can I say that when I haven't even had a proper conversation with him yet? And it's not a choice. Not yet."

She shrugs. "It's not weird to be attracted to someone you hardly know."

Something tells me she knows more than she's telling about that, and I want to get it out of her. I want her to be free to talk about anything with me from now on as well.

"Go on. Tell me." I wink and nudge her.

"Tell you what?"

"Who's the dude that's lucky enough to have you pining away over him? I know there's someone."

Her cheeks turn pink. "Oh, no one, really."

"Don't lie to me, Crystalline Maybelline Edwards." She cringes at my use of her full name.

"Okay, okay. He's one of Bryan's friends." She pauses for a few beats before going on. Bryan is her twin brother, and he doesn't always hang with the best company, I know that. "He's a bit older and Bryan only started hanging out with him recently. He totally looks like a surfer dude, blond hair and all."

My first reaction is concern and protectiveness, but I don't want to beat her down. "Well, in that case, I want to meet him sometime, and make sure he's good enough for a girl like you."

She smiles at me. "And I have to meet Aiden. He better be amazingly amazing to come close to even being deserving of you."

I smile at her choice of words and how happy she sounds. And I realize that I feel kind of happy myself, happy and hopeful.

Chapter 5 - Jealousy and a Red Dress

After December 31st (past tense)

CLEO

I had been planning on going to Adrianne's party, the big party everyone had been talking about for quite a while, but decided against it when I got home the Friday afternoon just before. I resolved to stay at home because of something that had happened earlier that day.

Since I had met Aiden, I hadn't been able to stop myself from thinking about him. I was irritated with myself for crushing so easily, but at the same time couldn't help myself. I really wanted to talk to him again, but felt too shy to say anything, not that I had many chances to anyways. It didn't stop me from wondering if he was thinking about me too, though, and thinking about whether we had had a connection or not. Cheesy, yeah, but I'm a cheesy sort of girl. Or so my older sister used to say when she was teasing me.

I had been thinking about him so often that I realized I was idolizing him. God gently reminded me that I should always put Him first, by using two verses that spoke to me very clearly while I was reading my bible before school that day.

The first was Matthew chapter six verse thirty-three, a verse I knew well but needed to hear again. "But seek first the kingdom of God and His righteousness, and all these things shall be added to you."

And then I came across verse five and six in chapter three of Proverbs. "Trust in the Lord with all your heart, and lean not on your own understanding; in all your ways acknowledge Him, and He shall direct your paths."

God was definitely speaking to me.

"Thank you, Lord," I spoke aloud as I so often did with God when it's just Him and me. "Thank you for knowing me and guiding me and loving me. You are the centrepiece of my life, you come first."

I made up my mind to get Aiden off my mind and replace him with God and all of His goodness.

It was going well, I felt closer to the Lord and just overall happier.

Until I saw something going on in the school hall on that Friday morning.

I saw Adrianne, leaning casually against the wall and batting her eyelashes up at none other than Aiden. The flirting was obvious. Aiden had his arm up against the wall and he was smiling down at her. I started walking faster. I kind of knew I had feelings for him, but I had no idea it would hurt this bad to see him being flirty with another girl.

As I walked past I heard Adrianne talking with a voice that dripped honey. "Of course you're invited. So don't disappoint me, Aiden, I'll be looking forward to seeing you there."

"Wouldn't dream of disappointing you," he returned.

I had to get away.

"Cleo?" Aiden was calling me back, although I had no idea why. Wasn't Adrianne one of the prettiest girls in school? He surely didn't want anything to do with me. I pretended I hadn't heard him and turn the corner quickly so that I disappeared from their sight.

I heard another faint shout from Aiden. "Cleo!"

But I was already lost amongst the other kids heading to their classes.

~ ~ ~

Before December 31st (present tense)

AIDEN

I wonder why Cleo ignored me. She must have heard me. I just wanted to say hi since I haven't spoken to her again since I met her.

"You know her?" Adrianne cocks one of her eyebrows up and I remember what I was busy doing.

Manipulating Adrianne to get an invite to the party wasn't too difficult. I just laid it on thick, grinning at her and telling her she was gorgeous. Leaning in a little too close, maybe. I felt bad, but I was ignoring it as best as I could. I'd have to let her know tomorrow at the party that I wasn't interested in her after all. She was a pretty girl, but I felt nothing.

I know that toying with her feelings is wrong. But she'll get over it easily, won't she? From what I hear there are plenty others who would gladly have her.

I snap out of my thoughts when she asks if I'm okay.

"Yeah. I kind of do know her...actually, no, not really. Do you?" I ask.

"Umm, okay. Yes, we're friends."

"Oh. Cool. Listen, Adrianne, I have to go, but thanks so much for the invite. Can't wait to you there."

"Can't wait either." She smiles at me prettily.

"See ya." My tone is light but inwardly I'm cringing at what a jerk I am as I walk away. Using her just to get another girl is a jerk move for sure.

~ ~ ~

EMMA

I'm in the kitchen helping mom make spaghetti and meatballs for dinner when my phone buzzes. I roll the last meatball and wash my hands before pulling it out of my pocket. It's Crystie.

Crystie: Guess what???

Me: What???

Crystie: I just heard from Mary that Cara said that Adrianne said that Aiden is coming to the party tomorrow.

I roll my eyes but I'm smiling. I start typing my reply.

Me: I don't have anything to wear.

Crystie: Don't talk rubbish. Coming over right now to help u pick an outfit.

Me: Ok fine, if u must...

But I feel excited. Mom notices my expression and smiles with me. "What's got you so happy, baby?" she asks.

"Oh, nothing. Crystie is coming over for a bit if that's okay."

She raises an eyebrow and looks at me, before she turns her concentration back to the tiramisu recipe she was looking at. "Sure, Em."

She's trying to act like she's not that curious, but I know she is. And I do want to tell her what's going on. Just not yet.

Later, in my room, Crystie is throwing stuff out of my closet. "I'm not cleaning this up, you know," I say, as I scroll through Instagram while sitting cross-legged on the floor.

"Of course you are," she retorts. "I'm going to make you look like a friggin' movie star, the least you can do is clean up your own clothes afterwards."

"Oh, so you're saying that I need your help to look like a movie star?" I put my phone down and tilt my head in a challenging gesture.

She turns to look at me, a mischievous look on her face. "Well..."

I narrow my eyes and try not to grin. "That's it. You're getting it." I grab the pillow off my bed and throw it at her. It hits her square in the face.

She looks a little surprised at first, but then her expression changes and she picks it up. I'm ready with my other pillow in my hands and as she starts to swing at me, I do the same.

We end up laughing till we cry on the floor with my room in an even bigger mess. I can tell we're both tired and need to sleep, but I want to stay awake and continue our pillow fight. It's been some time since I felt so carefree.

Crystie whacks me once more with the pillow which throws me onto my back on top of a pile of my clothes. I'm about to get up and return the attack, but then Crystie gasps.

"What?" I ask, still lying on the clothes.

"I don't remember throwing that one out."

She's looking behind me, and I lean forward so I can turn my head and see what she's staring at. I realize that Crystie is talking about my red spaghetti dress that I have only worn once. The fabric is soft and it's a classy cut. I received it in the mail from my uncle who lives in Virginia, he told me it was a very nice brand. He'd sent it with a note that said: Only the finest for my Emma.

"Wow," she breathes. "Put it on. Now."

I sigh. "Whatever you say, boss."

Minutes later I'm twirling in front of Crystie with the red dress on. "What do you think?"

"Perfect."

Suddenly the door opens, and Patty walks in. "What are you two do-" she pauses when she sees me.

"You're going to the party tomorrow after all?" she asks.

I nod. "How do I look?"

She says the exact same thing that Crystie said. "Perfect."

I feel warm as I smile at them. Not only warm, but actually pretty. When last did I feel this way?

Chapter 6 - The Truth

Before December 31st

AIDEN

There are more people than I thought there would be at Adrianne's party. It's like almost the whole school is here. Even though she has a huge house, it's still packed, and being squashed up against so many different people as I walk through the crowds is claustrophobic.

I just need to find Emma, then I'm planning to ask her if she wants to get out of here and go someplace else. Of course, we first need to have a real conversation together. I'm hoping I make a good second impression, and that she doesn't think I'm a weirdo for asking her to hang out with me straight away.

"Aiden!"

Just my luck. In a sparkling turquoise dress, Adrianne is flouncing over to me. I thought I could slip by unnoticed, but apparently not.

"It's great to see you here," she smiles and flutters her eyelashes.

I return the smile as I look down at her, but my heart isn't in it. Now I'm going to have to get out of this.

"Do you want something to drink?" she asks.

"Uh, no thank you," I say, eyeing first the beer in her hand and then other bottles of alcohol on the table. I don't drink, even though I have had the opportunity to on several occasions like now.

My parents have taught me from young that to drink a little now and then when you're old enough is alright, but underage drinking while I'm not responsible enough could ruin a lot of things for me. I can see Adrianne swaying a little bit. I wonder how many drinks she has already had and where her parents are.

"Awh c'mon," her voice slurs slightly. "Have a bit of fun with me."

I shake my head and try to grin, but it feels like a grimace. She grabs my arm and starts pulling me towards where there is a small clearing near the table of booze.

"Fine, don't drink. But tell me you know how to dance?" She gazes up at me with brown puppy dog eyes.

"I might." I say. Electronic music, the kind of music I hate, is blasting loudly and a bunch of other kids are dancing around the place.

"Stop playing hard to get," she giggles, putting her arms around my neck. "Shall we dance?"

"Adrianne, I think you're drunk...I don't know if- I mean, I don't think-"

"Shhh." A slender, manicured finger is placed on my lips, closing them. "Just dance."

"I've got to go find someone." Having her only inches away from me is dangerous, I can feel that the smell of her perfume and her closeness is beginning to work on me. I know it's my own fault, I got myself into this sticky situation. And now I really have to get out of it. I back off from her. "I'm sorry, Adrianne, but I don't like you in that way."

First surprise clouds her features, then realization as it finally gets through to her in her drunken state, and then anger, flashing in her dark eyes.

"You're just another player." she says, calmly at first. But it turns to shrieking with her next words. "Go away! Get out of here!"

She tries to shove me backwards and becomes more frustrated when she can't, she's not strong enough. "I hate you!" she screams. People are looking at us now.

"I'm sorry." I say quietly.

"No, you're not." She pierces me with a cold stare. "Get out. Now!"

"Adrianne, girl, come on. Let's go get you some water." Another girl steps out of the crowd of onlookers to put her arms around Adrianne. She's wearing a red dress and her long golden hair hangs loose. She glares at me as she pulls Adrianne away.

I'd know those blue eyes anywhere.

They belong to Emma.

~ ~ ~

EMMA

As soon as I get home, all I want to do is lay on my bed and cry.

After finally getting Adrianne to calm down and watching her fall asleep in her own bed, I left the party. Now, in my own room, I have time to think things through, and I don't like what I'm feeling.

I feel stupid. Regretful that I could even think that Aiden was different. Everyone heard Adrianne. He's a player.

I know I've only got myself to thank for getting my hopes up, for expecting something. I feel tears brimming but I won't let them fall. I will not cry over a boy I do not even know.

Suddenly there's a loud tap on my window that makes me jump. What on earth? Probably just something that fell off the roof. But no. There's a thud again, louder this time. Everyone else in the house is asleep, so it can't be Patty, Carpenter or Eddie. Or my parents.

Slowly I make my way over to the window to draw the curtain back and peer out. I gasp and fall back in shock at what I see. The curtain falls back in place as I land with a thump on the ground.

It's Aiden. At my house. How did he get here? Did he follow me?

I get up to open the curtain again. He's mouthing the words 'come outside' at me. All of a sudden, I'm angry. Angrier than I have reason to be, but it feels so right to be angry with him. I leave my room and storm down the hall to the front door. I unlock it and stomp outside to find him still waiting outside my window.

"You!" I yell. His head swivels from facing the window to meet my stare. "You are nothing but a conniving, sneaky, mean boy, who hurt one of my friends. I don't know why I even liked you!" As soon as the words come out, I clamp a hand over my mouth.

His eyes look startled. And at the same time...pleased? "You like me?" he asks.

"Liked you. Past tense." I say crossly. I'm cross with him because of who he has turned out to be, and cross with myself for letting something like that slip out. "Now go away. What did you do, follow me? Are you a stalker, too?"

He looks me up and down, slowly. I realize I'm in a flimsy blue tank top and my favourite checked pyjama pants. Not exactly what I would have wanted him to see me in a few hours ago. But I don't care right now. And I'm not afraid. I've been afraid of boys for a while now, and I'm unsure as to why I'm not with him, but I like the new confidence. When he doesn't answer, I walk over to him and prod a finger in his chest, hating that I have to lift my face to meet his gaze.

"Leave. Now."

As he looks down at me, I wish I hadn't come closer. The moonlight is doing strange things to his blue eyes, making them shimmer and dance. In one swift movement, he grabs my hand in his.

"It's not what you think," he says.

I try to wrench my hand away and fail. His grip is strong. "Oh really? Next thing you're going to tell me is that you're a nice guy and you actually care about Adrianne, right?"

"No," he states calmly. "I'm going to tell you the truth, though."

"Let go of me."

"Not until you hear me out."

I frown and lift my chin defiantly. "Why should I?"

"Because it's important," he returns in a tone just as taut.

I try to pull away again.

"I did it because of you, okay?" he says.

"Me? What do I have to do with you and Adrianne?"

"I turned her away because of you."

"Me?" I repeat again and it comes out as a squeak.

Aiden laughs at my confused face. "Yes. You. I don't feel that way about Adrianne, but I think I do about you." He must see the disbelief, because he continues. "I've never had a girlfriend, I'm no player. I'll be honest, it was cruel of me to use Adrianne just to get invited to the party, but I had to see you."

I just gape at him. "You're for real?"

"Never been more real." Gently he lowers my hand to my side and releases it. "Do you believe me? I'm sorry I made you upset. I want to start over. I want to get to know you properly, Emma Rayburn."

Chapter 7 - A Chance

Before December 31st

EMMA

I can feel myself melting a bit at the soft expression in his eyes. No, Emma. Turn around now. Leave him outside. All men are the same. All boys. The same. Don't let this Trojan horse enter the walls you have built up.

Feeling rebellious against my own common sense, I disobey the warning thoughts and stay a little longer. "Why should I believe you?"

"I'll prove it to you," his face looks sincere. "I'll do anything to prove it to you if you give me a chance to."

I want to. I realize in a heartbeat that I want to give him a chance. I want this to be a fairy tale and I want him to be my prince charming. Get real, I tell myself. He's just a good liar.

I force my eyes to roll. "Please. Cut the rehearsed lines and get out of here."

I turn and begin to walk back to the house but the sound of his deep voice stops me. "You take two sugars in your tea."

I spin around. "What?"

He smiles a little. "You take two sugars in your tea. Your laugh is the prettiest laugh I've ever heard. You like reading books set in the middle ages. Your favourite colour is pink. You have perfect handwriting. You talk to the odd kids at school, because you are kind."

My mouth is hanging wide open now, and I'm a little surprised that no bugs have flown into it yet, but mostly, I'm caught on the words he just said.

Aiden laughs. "Speechless? I hope it doesn't seem weird...I just...like to watch you."

Watch me? He's learned all of this just from watching me while at school?

When I still don't speak, he does. "I like all of those things about you."

"You like that I take two sugars in my tea?" I sputter.

He shrugs. "I have never been allowed sugar in my tea. Or in coffee. My mom is a health freak. I like that you don't care."

A giggle rises up in me, and soon I can't help but let it out. He grins back at me. When I'm done laughing, I step closer to him. "Since you've just weirded me out, I have my own weird question for you."

"Okay," he says.

"How tall are you exactly? My friend says you're just below six foot, but I reckon you're above."

We both can't stop our laughter now. I think we must be exhausted from a long week at school and then the party tonight, but it feels great to laugh like this.

"Six foot three," he finally replies after we both calm down. "Last I checked."

"I knew it. Crystie owes me ten bucks." I swipe a tear off my cheek and smile at him.

"So..."

"I think I'll give you a chance to prove yourself."

"You think?" he raises an eyebrow.

"I change my mind easily," I say in a cheeky tone. "See you on Monday." I start to leave again, but Aiden steps forward and grabs my arm.

"Can't I see you tomorrow?" he pleads.

I think quickly, but can't come up with any reason to say no. I was going to kick back and chill for the whole of Saturday. Still, spending it with Aiden might be fun.

"Where?"

"I could pick you up and we can go hiking," he suggests. "You looked amazing in that red dress, by the way."

"Thanks," I can actually feel myself blushing. "Sounds good. Spruce Peak?" I've been to Spruce Peak before but I can never get enough of the fresh air and crisp, colourful scenery.

"Anywhere you want to go."

"Okay. I'll see you tomorrow then. At..."

"Ten in the morning. Bright and early."

"Alright. I'll be looking forward to it..." I trail off. His face looks hopeful and I can't resist. "Only because I love nature," I tease.

He's not daunted. His eyes dance. "I know. You read a lot of books on nature as well."

So that's why he chose hiking.

"Stalker."

"Guilty as charged."

I shake my head. "Goodnight."

"Night, blondie."

We look at each other for a moment longer, and then I walk back up the porch steps and inside, locking the door after me.

~ ~ ~

CLEO

I watch Aiden walk away whistling. He must have walked here from Adrianne's house where the party is still in full swing, a few houses down the street. I had gone to bed early, but hadn't been able to fall asleep. So I slipped out of the house quietly and went for a stroll. I was walking along in the shadows when I heard a familiar voice.

It was Aiden, laughing and talking to someone. As I got closer, sticking to the shadows so that I wasn't seen, I saw them. Aiden. And Emma. Emma Rayburn. They were laughing a little hysterically and if I am any good at telling body language, it looked like neither of them wanted to leave.

I was a little shocked. Emma hates boys, everyone knows that. Hasn't dated since sixth grade. But I'm more hooked on the fact that Aiden is messing around with another girl. Emma must have no idea who she's dealing with. But I wasn't brave enough to intrude and tell her he's no good. Instead I stayed in the dark and watched them until they said goodnight and parted.

As Aiden is walking away, I start walking again, in the opposite direction. Jesus, help me not to feel jealous or angry. Help me not to make up my mind to do something I'll regret. Give me the peace only You can give and do give so freely. I move on slowly, listening to the occasional hoot from an owl and the breeze making the leaves in the trees rustle. After a while I feel better. It's just me, God, and the whispering trees out here. The atmosphere feels calm, and a deep calm settles within me as well.

I have good things stored up for you, I hear my Heavenly Father speak to my heart. I have a plan. Trust me.

~ ~ ~

After December 31st

AIDEN

Remembering that night, I'm scornful of my younger self. I was very selfish back then. I just decided I was in love, instead of stopping to think that I had better be serious or someone could get really hurt.

It could have been her silky blonde hair or the smell of her when she came near me. I wasn't very good at deciphering between real feelings and temporary desires as a boy. I know even now, though, that I wasn't wrong in thinking her special and unique. Even my sixteen-year-old self could recognize a beautiful soul. I just wasn't smart enough to see it was battered and broken too.

Chapter 8 - The Perfect Day

Before December 31st

AIDEN

I watch Emma as her bouncy ponytail flies back in the wind. She's half smiling as she takes in the view before her.

"I'll never get tired of this place," she says. I have a feeling that I won't, either.

We're quite high up on Spruce Peak and the air has become thinner and colder. But Emma's right, our surroundings are brilliant. I'm in awe of the life around me, of the bright reds, the different tones of orange and the warm yellows. The colours of fall at their fullest. Looking down from the height we're at, I see the trees that crowd ski resorts and quaint houses full of character, and the still green rolls of hill after hill covered in healthy grass.

Stowe is definitely a change. It's so different from the city of Homestead, where the best of the scenery would be a few palm trees beneath the blue sky.

Leaves crunch beneath our feet as we continue to stroll up the worn trail path. The silence is comfortable between us, but I don't mind when Emma's soft voice breaks it. "My family believes there's an Almighty God who made all of this."

I'm mildly surprised at her saying 'my family', excluding herself in the equation. "And you don't?"

"I did." She shrugs. "Not anymore."

It's quiet for a while until I decide to tell her. "Neither do I."

But evolution has always seemed daft to me, and I can't help myself from wondering- where did all of this beauty come from, then?

~ ~ ~

Underneath a big tree swamped in bold colour, we spread our picnic blanket and eat sandwiches and cookies. I pull a few leaves out of Emma's hair and she pretends to be angry, saying she put them there on purpose. I find out that she loves to tell the dumbest knock-knock jokes and can't help but laugh while watching her expressions and movements as she tells them. Tired from the long hike, we flop down onto our backs. I put my arms behind my head and embrace the feeling of contentedness I feel inside.

"Aiden?" Emma rolls onto her side to look at me and I do the same.

"Yeah, blondie?"

"Are you glad that you moved to Stowe?" she asks.

I think a moment before answering. It was tough moving away from everything I've ever known. But I know at the same time that I like it here, too. "Yes. Now that I've met you, I'm glad I moved here."

Her face transforms into one of her heart stopping smiles. "You're cheesy."

I laugh. "Can't help it. You have that effect on me."

"Well, don't worry. I don't mind cheesy."

"Good, because there's a lot more where that came from." I reach out to brush a cookie crumb from the side of her perfect, full mouth. She instantly flinches and backs off a little bit. "Sorry," I say.

She shakes her head. She looks like she wants to say something more, but decides against it. I leave it. I don't want to push her. Instead I pick up a dry, dead leaf and crush it between my fingertips, listening to the sound it makes in this world that seems utterly quiet other than the occasional bird chirp.

I almost startle at the sudden sound of Emma clearing her throat. "Today has been lovely. Thank you, Aiden."

"I'm glad you enjoyed it. I did, too." I get up and brush crumbs and little bits of leaf off my clothing. She stays laying on the ground, eyes closed in her lull.

"C'mon, lazy, we should probably start heading back." I prod her leg gently with my foot. "Don't want your parents mad at me for keeping you out late, although I wish neither of us had to go home."

"Then let's just stay. It's so perfect here. The trees, the fresh air. You." She shields her eyes from the sun as she looks up at me.

I gaze down at her, spotting a few light freckles on her nose that I hadn't noticed before. She sighs a little and stretches out an arm for me to pull her up. I take it, but quickly find it's a mistake as she pulls with all of her strength, bringing me down to the spot next to her. Suddenly she's up in a flash, touching my shoulder before she runs off.

"Tag. You're it." Her eyes are gleaming with playfulness and I can't help but grin at her childishness.

"Alright," I say, standing up. "Judging by how slow you were while we were hiking...it won't take me long," I joke with her.

Her eyes sparkle and her body tenses, ready to sprint. I start, as if I'm about to run after her, and she sets off running. I laugh until she realizes that I'm still standing in the same place. She stops running and turns to glare at me. And then I run, catching up to her before she even has time to turn around again. I pick her up, spinning her a little before setting her down. But I don't let go.

"Tag," I breathe. "You're it."

She holds my gaze for a few beats, and we stand there, two pairs of blue eyes staring into each other, my hands on her shoulders.

~ ~ ~

EMMA

Everything in me is screaming not to trust him. Not to feel this way about him. You just met him, they shout. You hardly know him, or where he's been, or what he's done. I ignore them, and lean into Aiden, dropping my head against his chest. He smells like pine and earth, but clean at the same time. I feel his hand rest on my upper back, and then the deep rumble in him when he talks.

"Let's get you home, Emma."

I realize I feel tired and melty, like I wouldn't mind being carried home. But at the same time I don't want this moment to end, I don't want this day to end. I lean further into his tall, solid form. I feel safe. It only lasts a few seconds. His hand moves up, brushing aside my ponytail to cradle my neck and I freeze, suddenly getting a hold of myself. I pull away quickly.

"Yeah. We should go now." I can't bring myself to meet his eyes again, so I start towards the picnic set up and begin packing everything back into the backpacks, a little hurriedly.

"Emma?" Aiden's voice breaks through my thoughts. He's busy folding up the blanket and putting it away.

"Yeah?"

"I want you to tell me if you ever feel I'm pushing you, and I'll back off. I promise."

At those words, I feel deeply touched. I can't help the thrill that comes from knowing he cares about whether things are happening too fast for me or not. And the warm feelings come rushing back. I nod and flash him a smile to let him know I understand. He smiles back. We finish packing and we're off again, heading back down Spruce Peak.

Later, we're almost at the end of the trail when I trip over a tree root, letting out a gasp. I land on my bottom, pain spreading up my right leg. "Ugh, I'm so clumsy," I mutter, knowing Aiden, being behind me, must have seen my ungraceful fall.

I get a bit of a fright when I feel strong hands on my waist, picking me up from behind. He lifts me and places me back on my feet.

"Ow!" I yelp.

"What? Did I hurt you?" Aiden is beside me now, concern in his eyes.

"No," I say. "My toe, I don't know if I broke it when I stubbed it, but it's really sore."

"I can carry you-"

"No, that's okay," I assure him, quickly. I don't want to be a bother, like a baby who can't walk on her own. Besides, I'm heavy. "I'll be fine."

I take another step and the pain shooting up through my foot confirms my lie. It's not only my toe. Aiden must see the look of discomfort on my face, because he doesn't ask, he just picks me up, backpack and all.

"Put me down," I order.

"What, and leave you for the bears?"

"The bears are probably already hibernating, if there are any," I huff. He's already moving on, me in his arms. I struggle against him but it's no use, he has an iron grip.

"Might as well enjoy the ride, because I'm not letting you hurt yourself further," he quips, helpfully.

"You'll get tired. I'm heavy."

He seems amused. "You can't weigh much more than my German shepherd back at home. His name is Jiro."

I groan dramatically. "Glad to know your dog and I have something in common." But I'm actually enjoying the sway as he walks, and finding it's easy to ignore the pain in my foot if I just concentrate on the warmth of his arms.

"You're much prettier than Jiro, I promise." I can hear that he's smiling.

We make it to his car and he puts me down, panting a little. German shepherd or not, it must be exhausting carrying another person after hiking for so long. We both get into the old blue Jeep and he chucks his backpack into the back. I look over at him.

He glances at me. "What?"

"Thank you. For today."

"Anytime," he says. "I just hope your folks aren't too mad that your hair is a mess, your toe is broken and your butt is covered in mud." His eyes hold a mirthful glint.

"You don't look great yourself, you know," I tease, talking about the sweat marks on his shirt and the way his auburn hair is flopping over his forehead in short, messy waves.

"But I feel great." He beams at me and starts the engine.

Chapter 9 - Bad News

Before December 31st

EMMA

When I get home I can feel the pleasant, warm flush that seeped into my face on the way back in the car, as Aiden and I sang along together to I Will Survive by Gloria Gaynor. He can't sing to save his life and we both canned ourselves laughing whenever he tried to reach a high note.

I'm walking up the stairs to the house when the door abruptly opens, and Carpenter appears in front of me on the top step. With his blond hair and sky blue eyes, people have often asked if we're twins.

"Emma, where have you been?" He looks so worried, I want to wrap my arms around him and tell him he never has to worry again because I've found someone who makes me happy. But I don't. Because although I want to be sure, I'm not, yet.

"I was out with a friend," I say, nonchalantly.

He frowns and closes the door behind him. "Was that friend," he uses his fingers to make air quotation marks, "the same boy that just drove away, by any chance?"

I shrug and give him an angel smile. "Maybe."

He runs a hand through his hair and it sticks out in weird places afterwards. "This isn't funny, Emma...don't tell me you've forgotten what happened last time."

This sort of protectiveness is the kind I hate. When he acts like I'm too dumb, naïve and wide eyed to make my own decisions anymore. I used to be, once upon a time, but surely he knows I'm far more grown up now?

"I don't need a reminder." I try to shove past him and he stops me, grabbing my arm.

"Please just be careful with yourself."

I simply nod and look down at my shoes, refusing to look him in the face. He sighs and drops my arm. "Well, I'm going to go see Jack. See you later."

I give him a quick hug to show him I appreciate his concern, and then watch him cycle away on his beloved Giant bike.

Once I'm inside my room, I toss my backpack on the bed and start undressing for the shower. There's a loud knock on my door while I'm busy taking my tank top off. I quickly pull it back down. "Come in!"

Mom opens the door and pads inside in her fluffy slippers. "Hey, Em. I have something to tell you."

I quirk a brow. "Good or bad news?"

She looks uncomfortable, and unhappy, like she doesn't want to tell me what she has to say. "It doesn't have to be bad if we go about it the right way."

"Okay..." I wait for her to speak.

She lets out a slow breath as if she's bracing herself. "Blaze Brooke has to come to town for a few weeks."

I freeze. I hear my heart thumping in my chest at the sound of his name, but not in a good way. I wonder if mom can hear it, I wouldn't be surprised if she could, it's reverberating so loudly inside of me.

"You remember his mother, Cherry Brooke. She was a lovely lady."

Yes, I remember her. I remember how Blaze used to say that her weak will and passiveness made him angry. Everyone else loved her, she was so sincere and kind to all, so I never understood why he felt that way. But then again, a lot of things made him angry. Something else mom said is also making my head reel with unwelcome thoughts and memories. Was a lovely lady?

Before I can ask, she explains. "Cherry recently passed away. Cancer. What with the way Blaze's father is, you know how he is, Blaze has to come back here to help arrange the funeral himself and of course attend. They are a bit low on funds, since they have to pay for the funeral, and one must keep in mind Blaze's studies and the flight here from Connecticut, so he can't afford to pay to stay somewhere...it's quite sad, that Brad Brooke won't allow his own son to stay with him-"

"I don't blame him at all," I bite out.

"Honey, please. Listen. Blaze has nowhere else to stay, he must stay with us. It's the Christian thing to do."

I feel anger flare. How can she do this, after everything? "The Christian thing to do is what stopped me from pressing charges against him!" I yell. "I agreed to it to please you. You said he had a future ahead and I shouldn't be the one to ruin it, because what would Jesus do, right? You told me to forgive. But this? This is too much; you must know that."

"Calm down, sweetheart." There's a determined look in her eye, and I know she won't change her mind. She cared very much for Cherry and probably just wants to honour her, but I honestly can't believe her right now. "You, of course, won't have to be here while Blaze is. You can stay with Crystie and her family, I've already asked them if it's okay."

"You're kicking me OUT? So that he can have somewhere to stay?" I feel flames in my chest, the fury and confusion constricting me, ruining the perfect day I had with Aiden. I thought she cared about me more than this.

"Emma-"

"No." I snap. "Don't Emma me. Does dad know about this?"

She presses her lips together. "Don't talk to me like that. Yes, he's not happy about it either-"

"You seem pretty okay about it," I spit out.

"Please, Emma. Listen to yourself. We're Christians, we're supposed to be a light in this world and turn the other cheek. Your father very much dislikes Blaze for what he did, but he also knows this is the right thing to do."

"Dislikes him? Hating him would be more appropriate. Tell me you hate him, mom. Because I do. And you're on my side, aren't you?"

She sucks in a breath. "Don't say that, Emma. The bible says that saying you hate someone is as good as murdering them."

"Yeah, well, I reckon I wouldn't mind him being murdered." I turn on my heel, walking into the en suite bathroom and slamming the door behind me. A thought comes to me and I spin around again, opening the door and stomping out. Mom stands exactly where I left her.

I want to shout, but the words come out as a whisper. "You are on my side, right?"

She walks over and wraps her arms around me. "Always, my strong girl. But I need you to do this. I know you can. Do you?"

I could scream. I could throw things. I could cry. All of those options run through my mind. I would like to do any of them, that's how much I don't know how to handle what I'm feeling. But mom is hugging me to her chest so tightly and her soft warmth makes me feel better. In my head I'm remembering who held me the night I was crying so much I couldn't see or breathe properly. And I realize my love for her is stronger than my hate for Blaze. Besides, if I don't have to see him, I might make it out alive.

"Yes," I decide, at the same time I say the word.

"That's my Emma." When I look up, her eyes are closed and her lips are moving silently in prayer.

I almost can't remember what it's like to pray. I feel a tug at my heart and I'm very close to giving in before I harden my will and manage to resist. Why pray to a God that allows awful things to happen to his supposedly loved children? Cherry Brooke was a devout Christian, and she ended up dying of cancer, sharing a home with a husband who never actually loved her and missing a son that wasn't worth being missed at all.

And me, well, I will never be able to forget Blaze either, or what he did, for as long as I try.

Chapter 10 - A Promise

Before December 31st

AIDEN

I eat lunch with Emma on Tuesday. I try to make her laugh the way I did on Saturday when we went hiking, but she seems withdrawn and quiet. I hate seeing her like this, her eyes look so sad and her shoulders slump slightly.

"What's wrong, Emma?"

She looks up from her salad. "Nothing? Why?"

"I'm not that dumb, Emma. I mean, I know it seems that way sometimes. But I can tell when something's up with you."

She smiles a little. "I'm fine. And you're not dumb."

On an impulse I leave my seat to sit down on the chair next to her, instead of sitting across from her, and put an arm around her. "So I'm not being dumb if I do this?" She shakes her head, a full smile taking over her face now as she looks away from me, shyly.

"What about this?" I tilt her chin to me with two fingers and before I can change my mind, I plant a quick, gentle kiss on her lips. She jumps back a little as if shocked. My lips are still tingling with electricity, but I sense that the kiss upset her.

"I guess that was dumb of me," I say. "I'm sorry. I should have asked."

Emma relaxes in her chair a little, like she was expecting my reaction to her surprise to be different. "It's okay." She looks down at her food and then at me again. "I just want things...to go slowly."

I nod. All I want to do is kiss her velvety lips again but I know I can resist for her sake.

~ ~ ~

EMMA

I don't want to tell him about Blaze, about the fact that knowing he will be here in October means my nightmares have started again. When Aiden kissed me, I couldn't help flashing back to when Blaze first kissed me. And even though Aiden was much more gentle, I thought about Blaze when our lips touched and I felt scared. Then, when I pulled away, I almost expected him to be furious with me, the way Blaze used to get if I denied him anything. He wasn't, and I immediately felt silly for being so uptight. But I had my reasons. By the time I pull myself out of my thoughts, I catch Aiden looking at me with a soft expression on his face.

"I don't mind if you don't want to talk about it," he says, as if he can read my mind.

"Thank you."

He looks at me with concern now and then as we finish eating. Concern... and something else, in his eyes, as they drop to my lips for a moment before quickly glancing away. I feel myself blush. I actually enjoyed the kiss, but the bad memories that came flooding into my mind were too much.

"Hey," he speaks suddenly. "Wanna bunk the rest of school and go someplace?"

"I've never bunked before." But I'm surprised to feel eagerness at the idea.

"Neither have I. But it seems to me that you need to go somewhere to get somethings off your mind." His voice lowers, on purpose or not I don't know. "So could I." When his cheeks colour a little, I catch his meaning and blush again as well.

"Okay. Let's. But where will we go?" I feel tingles down my spine, both from the kiss and from the excitement over bunking school.

He smiles broadly, any remaining blush disappearing from his face as his eyes take on a shine. "It'll be a surprise." He grabs my hand. "Let's go."

We manage to sneak out of the school in the busyness of lunchtime and run to Aiden's car as rain falls down on us in heavy plops. The sky is partly cloudy, but the sun is still shining even through the downpour. My hair is getting soaked. Aiden's hair is also pasted flat to his forehead, his burnt copper locks dark and dripping. I almost slip, because of the wet pavement and my still sore toe, but I grab onto his shirt and he supports me until I'm steady again. I laugh at my own clumsiness and so does he. We end up laughing all the way to the car. I'm revelling in just being a crazy, young kid bunking school. I realize that being able to feel younger and more innocent again is one of the best things Aiden could have done for me, and he has.

By the time we have reached our destination, which appears to be a small townhouse, the rain has let up. Aiden parks in the driveway and turns to me. "My mom makes friends pretty quickly, and even though we only moved last month, she's bonded with this old lady called Ella."

"Okay," I say, not sure why he's telling me this.

"Ella happens to have a hot air balloon." His smile is wide.

I'm not sure I'm following properly. "A hot air balloon?"

"Yeah. And she told my mom that she'd give a free ride to her kids sometime. So I figured, why not today?"

I'm still stuck on 'hot air balloon'. I have wanted to take a ride in one for ages, ever since the day I went to the Stoweflake Hot Air Balloon Festival at age nine. "We can? Won't she disapprove of us being out of school?"

"I guess we'll find out." He's already getting out of the car, so I follow suit.

We walk up to the door and Aiden raps on it. After a few minutes, when he's about to knock again, it opens and a friendly face peeps around. Ella wears round, old fashioned spectacles and has a cloud of white hair.

"Children, what a lovely surprise. Come in, come in," her voice tinkles.

We wipe our shoes on the doormat and enter. "Hi, Miss Ella," Aiden begins.

"Do call me El, darling."

"Okay...El, how are you?"

"Good, good. But something tells me that's not why you're here?" She casts a friendly glance at me where I stand a little bit behind Aiden. I smile back at her.

"Uh, no. I'm Sara Harper's son, Aiden."

"Nice to meet you, darling. And who is your pretty girlfriend?"

We both flush. "She's not my girlfriend," Aiden explains. "Although if I'm honest I'm hoping it might be that way someday."

Did Aiden just imply that he wants me to be his girl? Yes, he did. I snap out of it and hold out my hand to El. "I'm Emma Rayburn." She ignores my hand and pulls me into a hug.

"I can see why, young man. She really is lovely, isn't she."

It isn't a question, but he just nods and grins at me while I shift uncomfortably. I'm not sure how to respond to the warmth that washes over me whenever he looks at me like that. Like I'm fascinating.

"I s'pose you two are wanting a date in a hot air balloon?" she croons, apparently delighted at the notion.

"Not a date-" I'm busy saying, when Aiden interrupts.

"Yes. If you would be so kind? I'm willing to pay."

"No, no," El tuts. "No pay. It's enough just to see such young, clearly in love faces."

Even as my face heats again, Aiden's gaze slides to meet mine, and I feel the silent communication that passes between us. It turns something inside of me to liquid.

~ ~ ~

AIDEN

Emma's excited laughter makes me feel happy. She's leaning over the side of the basket looking down on all of Stowe. We're in the sky in El's rainbow air balloon that she calls Merry. She isn't with us, but her son, Martin is. Martin controls the hot air balloon while Emma and I ooh and ah at all there is to see. I'm once again amazed by the gorgeous place that I now live in. We pass over trees, old chapels with stained glass windows, and even a few waterfalls and lakes, as we float on.

When we land and it's over, the look in Emma's eyes is all I need to feel I've accomplished something. She grips my hand. "I have wanted to do that since I was little."

I feel something coursing through my body at the way her small hand fits into my bigger hand. "Then I promise it won't be the last time," I say.

She just smiles up at me. The haunted look in her face has disappeared.

For now.

Author's note: Hey guys! Thank you so much for reading this far. I wanted to say that any personal opinons, suggestions, advice or constructive criticism are/is more than welcome. Please comment your thoughts! Also, if you can point out any mistakes, don't be shy to do so.

And, for those of you who read the previous chapter before I changed 'Hunter' Brooke's name- I changed his name from Hunter to Blaze because it just felt like the better name for him, if you know what I mean. Sorry for any confusion caused.

What do you think of how things are going between Aiden and Emma? Too fast? Too slow? Let me know what you think.

Chapter 11 - A Dare

Before December 31st

AIDEN

Stupid history oral. Due on Monday. And, in Mr. Hardwell's own words, I'll be watching you closely, Harper. Which is just brilliant. I honestly don't know what I did to make him hate me so much, but he hasn't been making things easy for me.

If only I didn't have to study, I could be spending more time with Emma. But I do, because my parents are not the kind of parents that will give their son a hug and tell him well done for trying if he fails. They won't murder me or anything, they'll just shake their heads, faces full of disappointment, and tell me I can do better. I can't stand disappointing them, the way it made me feel when they approached me about bunking school on Tuesday was enough to remind me why I haven't before.

Garth, on the other hand, gets bad grades all of the time and his parents don't seem to mind too much. Or, if they do, Garth doesn't act like he cares a lot about it. Tempting him the only way I know how, I insist that all the girls like smart dudes, and drag him with me to the library to study on Saturday afternoon.

"Ugh," he groans as he flips through an old, dusty encyclopaedia. "I hate books. I can't believe I let you talk me into this. I thought you were cool, but if you were you wouldn't force your buddy into coming to a library to hangout."

I smile and roll my eyes at his drama. "If you find reading so boring, here's an idea. I dare you to talk to that girl." I nod in the direction of a girl sitting at the table in front of us. Her back is turned to us and all we can see is her long, wavy brown hair. She's bent over, reading something. She must be so absorbed in her book that she didn't notice us come in. No one else is in this section of the library, it seems that the rest of the world didn't think it a wonderful idea to visit the library on a Saturday.

Garth's eyes dart to the girl and then back to me again. "And say what?"

I shrug, holding back a chuckle at him actually considering it. "I don't know. Ask her name, for starters." I return my attention to the book on WWI that I was reading.

"Is that how you got Emma talking to you? You just asked her name?" Garth interrupts my concentration.

I sigh. "Nope. There was more to it than that."

"Like what?" he asks. "Everybody is amazed, including me. Do you know how long Nathan Park has been trying to get her to go out with him? And he could have any girl he wants."

"Dude. Seriously, Nathan Park isn't me," I tease, and quickly deflect the play punch to my shoulder.

"If I talk to that girl, will you tell me?"

I shake my head. "If you get that girl's number, then I might give you more details."

He narrows his eyes. "Fine."

He doesn't waste anytime dumping the encyclopaedia on the table and leaving his seat. Strolling up behind the brunette girl, he taps her shoulder. She jumps, spinning around to look at him.

Then I recognize her.

It's Cleo.

~ ~ ~

CLEO

The tap on my shoulder gives me a huge fright. I turn and find myself looking at a boy with sandy blond hair that flops over his forehead and warm brown eyes peeking out from beneath. Do I know this guy?

"Hi," he says.

"Um, hi."

"I'm Garth," he holds out a big hand and I shake it with my own, still very confused. My bewilderment increases when I notice someone else in the room, looking at me from the table behind me.

Aiden.

Garth clears his throat and my eyes jerk back to him. "You have really beautiful eyes," he comments, casually and leans forward a bit. Is he flirting with me?

"Uh, thanks," I reply. I can feel my cheeks warming.

"So...I know this might be a little weird, but, uh, can I have you number?"

What? I look to Aiden and then to Garth again. Are they playing some sort of prank on me? Probably. Aiden hasn't given me a second glance since the day I met him, so I doubt he'd care much about me being pranked.

"Why?" It feels dumb to ask, but I don't want to walk straight into something.

"Well..." Garth looks a little nervous now, rubbing the back of his neck as he looks down at me. "I want to go on a date with you sometime."

"You don't even know my name."

"What's your name?"

I can't help rolling my eyes. "Cleo."

"Nice name. So, about the number..." Garth lets the sentence trail on.

I realize Aiden is still staring at me, and he hasn't spoken a word. Then a thought strikes me. If, which is a very big if, if Aiden cares anything for me, accepting Garth's proposition of going on a date might make him jealous.Wait, slow down, Cleo. Didn't you see him with Emma the other night? He wouldn't get jealous over you, you're the only one who's been getting jealous.

But Garth is nice looking and he seems friendly enough. It wouldn't only be about trying to get back at Aiden. I ask myself, is it a yes or no? I've only been asked out once before.

And the last person to ask me out was my best friend. Before I said no to him.

I still think about him often. Daniel Farley. It was a year ago and we've long since drifted apart. I felt bad that turning him away romantically ending up meaning the end of our strong friendship. He couldn't take being around me after that.

If I close my eyes I can see his bright green eyes, golden skin and light brown hair.

Daniel is different now. He stopped coming to church a while ago. He drives a Harley Davidson bike and has that classic bad boy image about him, getting with all the girls, beating up any guys who cross him. He got a piercing in his left ear and a tattoo recently, or so I heard. All of this I've been told by his cousin, Jacki, who lives next door to him.

I just remember him as the kid with a head of curls and a big smile.

I miss when it was simple, when we were kids and just friends. Sometimes I resent that he had to go and complicate things. But I know that the way I handled it wasn't exactly done in the best way, and I regret it.

Now here I am, faced with the same question again, this time from someone I hardly know compared to someone I've known my whole life. I force myself out of my thoughts and stand to attention. Garth's friendly stance and carefree aura is contradicted by his facial expressions. He looks doubtful over what he just got himself into and a little impatient as he waits for my answer.

"Um," I murmur. Against my better judgement, I make a decision weighted by the fact that I want to see where this goes. I want to see if Aiden cares or not, despite telling myself that's not true, I know it is.

"Okay. Sure. You can have my number."

Out of the corner of my eye I see Aiden's frown.

Author's note: Hey! Thanks for reading, I really appreciate it. Hope you didn't find this chapter too short or too boring. I'll try to keep the next chapter longer.

What do you think of Cleo giving Garth a chance? Do you think she harbours any left over feelings for Daniel?

Chapter 12 - Daniel

Before December 31st

AIDEN

I can't believe it. Firstly, I didn't expect Garth to actually follow through with the dare. Secondly, I most definitely wasn't expecting the girl to be Cleo.

But the surprise that hits the hardest is feeling whatever it is that's working its way inside of me. It's the kind of feeling I should only be having for Emma. It's a mixture of envy and protectiveness for Cleo, and even irritation towards Garth at the same time.

Come on, I tell myself, think about Emma. I should be thinking about Emma, not worrying over Garth taking Cleo out or something stupid like that. I hardly know Cleo. And she hasn't made it seem like she wants to get to know me, either. So why do I feel so...cheated?

My thoughts fall back to Emma. I have been planning to ask her out properly. I don't want everyone to just assume we're together, that's too flimsy. I want it to be official. But I also want it to be perfectly set up when I do ask, so I've been trying to come up with the right way to do it. Judging by the way Garth is gazing at Cleo, he won't be much help. This is something else I was not expecting- Garth falling head over heels for her already. For some reason it makes me uneasy and my stomach churns. They just met! I thought Cleo was a girl with more wit about her than that. A small voice nags at me inside my head. Hypocrite. You have only had one conversation with Cleo and just look at the way you feel. And let's not even start on the way you went about getting to know Emma.

It's all so confusing that I'm getting a headache. I know I'm attracted to Emma, not only her physical appearance but her personality, too. But there is something about Cleo that draws me in, almost like there's a mystery about her that wants me to unravel it. How am I ever going to figure this out? I put a palm to my forehead and groan out loud, without meaning to.

"You okay?" Cleo's voice drags me out of my thoughts. She's looking at me with concern in her magnificent green eyes.

"Huh?" I feel a bit dazed and my headache is only getting worse. "Oh yeah, I'm fine. But I should get going, so I'll see you both around. Enjoy that date." I direct my wink at Garth and force myself to act nonchalant and carefree, as if it couldn't mean less to me if they go out together.

Swinging my backpack over my shoulder, I leave the library without looking back.

~ ~ ~

On Monday morning I still have a headache. I didn't sleep well the past two nights and I'm unsure whether my oral is going to impress Mr. Hardwell or not. Nothing I do impresses him really, so I guess there's no need to get my hopes up.

On my way to history class, I bump into Cleo again, in the same place as I did when we first met. Except this time, I don't bump into her physically, rather, I come across her and another guy in the hall. The dude is almost my height and wearing a tank top that reveals the tattoo he has of an eagle in flight on his left arm. He also wears a glinting silver stud in his right ear. He's talking in a low, menacing tone to Cleo and she's shrinking back from him against the wall. There's confusion in her eyes and her small frame is tense. It's clear he's trying to intimidate her, and I feel anger rise inside of me at the sight of it. Before my mind can process what my body is doing, I pace forward and place myself between them.

~ ~ ~

CLEO

It's just a normal Monday. Other than the fact that my thoughts keep on drifting to the whole Garth situation. I wonder when and if he is actually going to take me out. And I wonder at Aiden's reaction to the whole thing- he seemed to not care at all. I couldn't deny that it made me disappointed, but I ignored that. It wasn't the first time he'd disappointed me anyway, I should really stop expecting more from him. Garth and I get on well enough. He isn't as sharp as Aiden seemed to be, but he is easy to be around. Still, something inside of me says that's no good reason to move too quickly with him.

I'm walking down the school hall, my mind wandering far away as I clutch my books to my chest, when all of a sudden a voice all too familiar rings out, crashing through my thoughts.

I stand still in my tracks, frozen.

Daniel?

I blink, and realize it is him. He's standing in front of me. He seems to have gotten so much taller than when I last saw him, when we were both almost fifteen. His hair is the longest I have ever seen it and I notice that the rumour I heard about him having a tattoo is true. It's a soaring eagle on his left upper arm. Something comes to me, and I remember Daniel's favourite bible verse from back when the name Jesus would still make him excited.

"But those who wait on the Lord shall renew their strength; they shall mount up with wings like eagles, they shall run and not be weary, they shall walk and not be faint."

Isaiah 40:31.

I ponder for a split second if the tat could be linked to the verse, but only for a moment, before he says my name again.

"Cleo!" He's almost yelling. "I'm talking to you, so stop your daydreaming. You always did get your head stuck in the clouds easily."

I flinch at his tone. "Daniel. Long time no see. I thought you were still in Massachusetts." His parents are divorced, and he's been living with his dad in Massachusetts for a while. Or so I thought. I haven't had contact with him for a long time now. I used to try messaging him, but he never replied, so I gave up.

"Well, I'm back, so now I'll be around to remind you of what you could have had." His grin is arrogant, his stance hostile yet boastful, and I can't place his demeanour as that of the boy I used to know. "Miss me much?"

I want to say yes. Yes, Daniel, I've missed you so much. But not this fake person, not this mask, this façade. I miss the real Daniel. But I know it's better to just shut my mouth about that and move on. "I have to go. Maybe I'll see you around." My body feels stiff and uncompliant as I force myself to start walking away.

But Daniel is having none of it. He takes one big step to the right to block my way and I find myself backing off, pressing up against the wall.

I take a deep breath and try to keep my voice quiet and firm. "I need to go, Daniel."

"After all this time? You wanna act like nothing happened?"

"No. Something did happen, but it won't do any good going back there now. It's in the past." I honestly hadn't thought that he was mad at me. Upset, yes, upset enough to end our friendship, I know that. Sad, maybe. But I hadn't realized that he was furious, like he seemed to be now. At the back of my mind I'm wondering if it's really me he's mad at, or if there's something else that's going on. But I'm too nervous to ask, so I try to push past him again.

I feel a burst of surprise and a gasp escapes when he grabs my shoulder and shoves me back. He has never treated me, and as far as I know, any other girl, so roughly like that. He wouldn't. Or, the Daniel I knew wouldn't. This seems to be a different Daniel entirely.

"What happened to you," I say, under my breath. It comes out as more of a statement rather than a question.

"What?" He leans forward, his eyes narrowing. I swallow and decide not to repeat what I said.

"Please let me pass, Danny." I use the name I used to call him when we were kids, hoping it will soften the shell he's hiding beneath. But I see that it's a mistake when his eyes harden.

"Do not call me that." He clenches his jaw. "You lost the right to call me that."

I feel a flash of indignation. Before I can convince myself it's wiser to bite my tongue, I counter with, "Do you really think I was the one who ruined things? Because I think you and I both know that isn't the truth." He just glares at me and doesn't say anything, his nostrils flaring slightly. I hold my books closer to me protectively, preparing to go on. "What, or who, has you worked up like this? It isn't me."

"You think you know it all!" His shout makes me jump and almost hit my head on his chin, he's so close. "But you have no idea-"

"Hey, man." Suddenly Aiden has come out of nowhere and pushed his way in front of me. He faces Daniel, his shoulders rigid and his voice tight with held in temper. "Back off."

From behind Aiden, I see Daniel's face change from surprise to irritation, and then darken with anger. Judging by the way he's making fists out of his large hands and how his skin tinges red, this can't end well.

Author's note: Hey! Thanks for reading! I worked for a while on this, editing and re-editing it but after days of trying to get it right, I still don't feel it's quite there. I'd love to know your thoughts, though. Feel free to comment and let me know what they are, and vote if you enjoyed it.

I felt it was time I introduce Daniel. And although doing it in this way doesn't portray him in the best of lights, I'm working on building his character and this just needs to be a part of it.

What do you think about Aiden and Cleo's confusion over each other? And do you reckon that Daniel has a bigger, more serious reason for the way he acted towards Cleo?

Chapter 13 - Bruises

Before December 31st

DANIEL

I'm not even sure I intended to act so meanly towards Cleo, and in such an uncalled manner, too. But it's easy to leave that at the back of my mind as I stare into cold blue eyes.

Who is this guy anyway? Cleo's boyfriend? The person she chose over me? Doesn't matter. I don't care anyways, not anymore, I tell myself. But I can feel my muscles tensing of their own accord, and I know I'm ready to lash out and show him how I feel. He senses it, and spreads his legs further apart, planting himself firmer. His unwavering glare does nothing to quench the fire I feel inside of me.

"Aiden," Cleo says. Her voice is irritatingly calm. "It's okay. We were just talking, and I was just about to leave." She reaches from behind to touch his shoulder but he merely shrugs her off, holding eye contact with me. It's obvious she isn't going to convince him.

Good. You want a fight? I'll give you a fight. It won't be my first and I doubt it will take place as my last.

All the emotion I've been keeping pent up inside over the past few weeks is threatening to escape through my fists, and I let it, swinging a punch to Aiden's jaw. I see in his face that he's caught unaware, as if he wasn't really expecting me to throw the first punch. But he reacts quickly, blocking my jab and aiming one from beneath my chin.

"Stop!" Cleo's plea is faint compared to the sound of adrenaline rushing through me.

I jump out of the way and dodge his throw, before hitting my mark with my next punch. He doubles over for a second, cradling the hard blow to his abs. Straightening up and recovering fast, he hits my nose squarely with his clenched hand, and I hit his face as well in the process.

It actually feels good to be in a fight again, as if something inside of me is only released when I use my fists. I poise myself for another attack.

But it's over as abruptly as it started, when an enraged man wearing glasses walks out of a nearby classroom and yells at us. "Both of you stop it, now! Right now!"

Although I don't want to, I stand back, and so does Aiden. I can feel blood flowing from my nose. I glance fleetingly at Cleo, who stands wide eyed, her hands white from holding her books so tightly. Her eyes meet mine before I look away quickly. I don't want to see what she thinks of me now, as if what she must have thought already isn't bad enough. Regret is already starting to set in, the way it always does once the thrill of the fight is over.

"Mr. Hardwell." Aiden nods at the man, in between heaving. I must have hit his stomach harder than I thought, and I can't help the satisfied feeling that passes through me at knowing that, even if my knuckles ache already.

Hardwell is fuming. His face has almost turned purple. "Harper! I warn you, this school does not tolerate this kind of behaviour. It's...disrespectful! Scandalous! Irresponsible! Kids these days, they never think before making stupid decisions, and you two are no exception." He turns his glare away from Aiden to pierce me with it. "And you! What's your name, boy?"

"Daniel," I grunt, unwillingly.

"Full name!"

"Daniel Farley," I scowl. The blood has made its way down to my lips now, and I cringe inwardly from the metallic taste.

"Harper and Farley, I assure both of you that you will be spending the afternoon in the principal's office! I knew you were bad news, Harper."

Cleo is watching the whole thing, looking from Mr. Hardwell to Aiden, to me. Is it just me or does her glance linger on me longer than either of them? I feel a twinge of guilt at how I spoke to her. In truth, I just want to pull her into a hug. She looks a frightened and I feel my gut wrench at the fact that it's my fault.

"As for you, young lady, what was your place in all of this?" Hardwell directs his attention to her.

"Nothing. She had nothing to do with this." I say. Feeling defensive and protective of her takes me by surprise. Wasn't I angry with her just now?

But deep down inside, I know I never stopped caring about her in this way. I will never let anyone hurt her as long as I can help it. Yet I hurt her myself, badly. Not only today, but also when I abandoned our friendship. I haven't been around to make sure no one can hurt her. It must have seemed to her that I never looked back, but she probably has no idea that a day didn't pass by without me looking back.

"You can keep quiet, Mr. Farley. The girl can answer for herself." Hardwell frowns at me before turning back to Cleo. "Now, I'll ask again, were you involved?"

I suck in a breath and grit my teeth. Cleo is way too honest. She'll want to take part of the blame too, she wouldn't want to see us bear it alone when in her mind it's her fault.

"Yes, Mr. Hardwell. I..." She falters for a moment. "...well, it sort of started because I-"

I quickly interrupt her. I knew she was going to try and take it on her own shoulders. "It's my fault. She just saw it happen." I don't care if Aiden gets away easy and I take the full punishment myself, as long as Cleo doesn't have to. "I started it."

Hardwell still looks irritated with my intervening, but must be pleased with the confession, because he gives a curt nod. "Both of you may now make your way to the principal Wilson's office. I'll be in shortly to tell him of your foolishness."

Aiden and I stand still, both of us hesitant to follow an order given in such a haughty tone. But we start walking when he barks, "Move!"

I hear him telling Cleo to get to her class as we head to the principal's office.

It's my first day back at school in Stowe. I only got back from Massachusetts last week, because of a falling out I had with my dad. He told me it was best I stay with mom for a while, and now here I am. In Massachusetts, I got expelled from two schools within a matter of six months. The second time led to the huge fight I had with my dad.

I can't afford for anything serious to happen here, if mom also doesn't want me around, where will I go?

But here I am, on my first day at school, getting into a fight.

I look to the right out of the corner of my eye at Aiden. His face is grim. I can see a bruise starting to bloom on his face already.

He's probably a goody two shoes, never been in a fight, always gets good grades, has a clean record. Unlike me. No wonder he isn't happy about this.

No wonder Cleo likes him.

Quickly, I dismiss the thought. You don't know that. But if you did, it wouldn't matter to you.

Would it?

~ ~ ~

CLEO

I feel awful. If I'd stayed more relaxed, Daniel probably wouldn't have reacted the way he did, and Aiden wouldn't have felt he had to help me out.

Now they're both in trouble.

Lord, please may principal Wilson be kind in his disciplining, may the consequences not be too serious.

After my quick prayer, I try to concentrate on what my math teacher, Mrs. Howard, is saying. It's difficult. Partly because I hate math, but mostly because I keep on thinking about Aiden and Daniel.

~ ~ ~

AIDEN

Two weeks of detention after school, Mr. Wilson said. Well, for me. For Daniel it's three weeks, because he started it. They take physical violence very seriously, he said. And if we were to do it again, he'd give us a warning, and after that, one more slip up would mean being expelled.

My parents won't like it. But it's worth it. I wasn't going to allow Daniel to treat her like that, no one should. My eyes flicker to him, sitting next to me. His jaw is set, his eyes steely, staring straight ahead. But he leans back casually in his chair, arms behind his head, as if he doesn't care about the whole thing.

Pain throbs in my stomach and left cheek, but I'm not about to let it show. Besides, it's a good kind of pain. At least I know I fought for a worthy cause.

When we're finally allowed to leave the principal's office after Mr. Wilson's big speech on respect and responsibility, I find Emma waiting for me outside. I wonder if Cleo told her? Do they even know each other?

She rushes to me, eyes big. "Aiden, are you okay?" she asks.

Daniel looks at Emma and I think I see recognition flash in his eyes before he turns his face to me, giving me a cold look, one that says this isn't over. I have a feeling I just made an enemy. He wastes no time in grabbing his backpack, shrugging on his hoodie and leaving us, bumping his shoulders against mine briefly and purposely as he does. I ignore it and focus on Emma, who glares at Daniel's back.

"Yeah, I'm fine." I reply.

She reaches up and skims my cheekbone lightly with her finger where the bruise must be. I wince but don't back off, because I like the feel of her soft skin on mine.

She frowns at the retreating Daniel again. "I knew that kid. Daniel," she says.

I cock a brow. So I was right about him recognizing Emma. "Really? Knew?"

She lets out a soft sigh. "Yes. But it's a long story." Just like that, she effectively closes the subject.

"Well, let's get out of here," she suggests. "Detention only starts tomorrow, right?"

I nod. "Get out of here and go where?"

Emma offers me a grin that lights up her face. "It'll be a surprise."

Author's note: Thank you for reading :) I really appreciate it. Any comments and votes are appreciated too.I hope to have chapter fourteen ready soon. Oh, and a few days ago I finally put the cast up, so enjoy that!

Quick question: do you prefer using your imagination, or do you like it when there's a cast?

Chapter 14 - The Nightmare Returns

Before December 31st

EMMA

"Emma!" The voice echoes in the walls of my mind. Is it Blaze? Aiden? Something tells me the masculine voice is familiar, but I can't quite figure out who it is. "Emma, wake up!" I'm shaken, back and forth, back and forth. It must be Blaze. He's probably going to kick me now, or near strangle me, like he did before. "Emma!"

I sit up, gasping. Carpenter is in front of me, on my bed. It's so dark I can barely see his face- only his eyes gleam a light ocean colour in the blackness. Slowly, my vision adjusts and my breathing comes more regularly.

"Another nightmare?" Carpenter asks. "You were screaming bloody murder."

I nod, wiping sweat from my forehead. I'm still trembling a bit. Carpenter's tense expression softens and he draws me to his chest. "It's fine now," he says. "You can go back to sleep."

My brother's room is the closest to mine, it's no wonder he heard my howling. I'm thankful for the warmth and comfort that he is as I lean into him, sighing. After a while my eyes droop shut, and Carpenter hums to soothe me.

"Thanks, Carp," I murmur, before I feel myself fade away.

When I wake up in the warm rays of light streaming through from my bedroom window, I realize with a start what today is. Saturday. But I guess it's not really what today is that's bothering me, it's tomorrow.

Tomorrow, Blaze is coming back.

I'm moving in at Crystie's today. Mom told me she's not entirely sure how long Blaze will have to stay, but it's probably going to be at least three weeks, maybe more.

I stretch, trying to put all thoughts of Blaze Brooke out of my mind as I get up from my bed. I almost step on Carpenter when I do. He's lying on his side on the floor, snoring softly with his head on his pillow and my extra comforter covering him. He must have stayed in case I had another nightmare.

Oh, Carp. He's a real softie inside even though he tries not to let it show. I'm so grateful for him.

I step over him and tiptoe to the bathroom to get changed. When I get back he's awake, sitting up and rubbing his bleary eyes.

"Morning," he slurs. I stop myself from giggling at his loud yawn and obvious sleepiness. He never has been a morning person.

"Good morning," I say cheerfully. Apparently too cheerfully, because he raises a brow cynically.

"You sure you're ready for all this?" he croaks. By all this, I know he means me moving out and Blaze coming back.

"Yeah." I force a smile. "What about you? You're the one who's going to have to live in the same house as him for now."

He frowns a little. "I'll be fine. I'll be keeping an eye out for Patty and Eddie. He might get one of them in trouble or hurt if I don't. I can't trust Blaze, not at all."

"I know." Concern etches itself into his face at the two words I whisper, and I know he's remembering all that happened.

"We'll see each other at school and at church," he says, changing the subject for me.

I smile genuinely this time. "Never thought I'd say this, but I'll actually be looking forward to seeing you." He tosses his pillow at me and I dodge it. "I'm too fast for you." I stick out my tongue and run out of the room, with him chasing after me, clumsily because he's still sleepy.

~ ~ ~

My phone beeps while I'm busy packing up my clothes. It's Aiden, he sent through the photo he took of me on Monday when we went to McDonalds.

When I was younger and any of us had a bad day, my parents would pack my siblings and I into the car and head to McDonalds to get happy meals and then ice cream afterwards. Taking Aiden there after his fight with Daniel and sharing the family tradition with him almost felt like I was inviting him into our family.

I didn't ask him what the fight was about, but I still want to. Maybe I will, when I see him on Thursday. He's taking me, Crystie and her brother

Bryan to do some early Christmas shopping and just hangout for a bit at the mall after school. The thought came to me when I was talking to Crystie over the phone last night- I want Aiden to meet Bryan, who needs a friend that doesn't drink and smoke and all that other stuff. Crystie and I both worry about him sometimes. Plus, I want to get Aiden something for Christmas. I already have an idea. And I guess I could use some distraction from what's happening as well.

I smile at the photo on my phone. He captured a most flattering pic...not. My eyes are cross-eyed and I'm taking a huge bite of the burger. I can't help laughing at the memory of giggling with Aiden over the mess I made, on my chin and on my clothes. He wasn't much better himself, staining his shirt when he ate his own burger. Boy, he could eat a lot. He finished my ice cream for me when I couldn't and then we sat there, content and happy in each other's company, bellies full of McDonalds.

"I love your family already," he'd said, after I explained the tradition to him.

I had smiled down at our entwined fingers. He was rubbing his thumb along my knuckles. I marvelled at the way our hands fit so perfectly together and how safe I felt when he held mine. "I think they'd like you."

And I don't think I'd mind having him be a part of our family at all. Maybe one day. My heart flutters at the thought.

He's so different from Blaze. He's kind, gentle, thoughtful. The opposite, really. So why did I hold onto Blaze for so long?

Ugh. Stop thinking about Blaze. Just pack and get to Crystie's so that you can have a girls' night and forget about him.

More than anything, I want to forget about him. But it's going to be difficult, since he's going to be living in the same town as me for almost a month. At least I won't have to see him.

I shake my head and try to concentrate on packing.

Once I'm done, I decide to wait outside in the sunshine for Aiden to pick me up. All I told him was that I need to move out because there isn't enough space in the house for our guest unless I do. A little white lie, so what. I'm not ready to tell him the truth about Blaze, yet. Or the truth about why I won't be able to stand staying in the same house as him.

Aiden offered to take me to Crystie's, since dad took the only car we have to his workplace. But first, I want him to meet my mom and my siblings. They've heard about him, and I know that they've been worrying about me. Especially dad. He blames himself for what happened between Blaze and I, even though he shouldn't. It makes me sad to know that he does, it wasn't his fault at all. Not his fault that he didn't see what was going on. It was my fault for hiding it so well.

And Blaze's fault for doing what he did.

But I want to show them what a good guy Aiden is. How unlike Blaze he is.

Patty said nothing when I told her that I really liked him, she seemed to go into a trance or something. When I shook her back to reality, she simply said, softly, "I'm glad," and that was it.

She isn't home. When I told her I wanted her to be around to finally meet Aiden, she had said she already had plans, and gave me an apologetic smile.

"I want you to be careful, Em," she said, before leaving my room. Exactly what Carpenter instructed when I first told him about Aiden. But I suppose that's to be expected.

Carpenter, Eddie and mom are here, so I'll be able to introduce them to Aiden. I feel kind of nervous about it, actually. What if they don't like him?

It won't matter. All that matters is that I do.

I lie back on the green grass, my bags next to me, and think about the day we went hiking. I love to replay that day in my head over and over again.

Suddenly, I notice a car driving up the street. I sit up and jump to my feet, expecting it to be Aiden. But then I pause. Aiden drives a blue Jeep, not a black Ford.

My body stiffens when I see who is in the driver's seat.

I should go inside; I should get away. Quickly. But my feet seem to be glued to the lawn as he pulls up in the driveway, opens the car door, walks over to me.

And then he's standing there, right in front of me.

Even taller and bigger than I remember. Better looking too, if that's even possible, since he was always a looker. Dark brown, soft looking locks of hair. Gold flecked hazel eyes. Straight nose, full lips. Broad shoulders and biceps that show through his fitted long sleeved shirt.

Blaze is back.

Author's note: Hiii. So, I guess that was a little bit of a cliffhanger... ;) Thank you for reading! And listen, I really really really would appreciate you pointing out any mistakes or anything that doesn't seem right and telling me what you thought of this chapter.

So please, comment. Vote. Give that feedback that I love recieving. Also, have a lovely day and happy reading. ♥

Chapter 15 - Blaze

Before December 31st

BLAZE

Emma stands as still as a statue. In fact, she probably could have fooled me, if she didn't take a wobbly step backwards and almost fall. Instinct makes me reach out and catch her before she does.

Gripping her shoulders, I pull her upright but I don't let go. I can see her swallowing and her eyes dart around, looking anywhere but at me.

"Emma," I say. Finally, she fixes me with a look. I know that look. It's Emma trying to be brave.

So, she's still scared of me.

"What are you doing here? I thought you were only coming tomorrow."

"Guess I got here early. Miss me?" I grin. Her face twists a little and I wonder what's going through her mind.

She tries to shrug my hands off. "Stop touching me," she orders. But I still don't let go.

I honestly couldn't explain it if I tried to. The way I want to make someone feel as small as my dad made me feel. The need to make them feel all the pain, the frustration, the helplessness.

And Emma was that someone. Is still that someone, if the way she's shaking like a leaf beneath my touch is any indication. Too small and defenceless to do anything about it, just the way I was when my dad would beat me with a cricket bat as a young boy. When he would yell about how useless I was, about how he couldn't believe he was stuck with a son like me.

But it was worse when he would hit mom. She never told anyone, she covered up the bruises with makeup, and she took it. She just took it.

It made me angry, her silence. Her enduring. I wanted her to fight back for us, to fight for and with me, but both of us were too afraid to do that. And it's no wonder.

I remember the night dad threw a vase, flowers and all, at my head. I remember mom screaming and wailing for him to stop. I remember how the next morning dawned with my head hurting so bad I thought I would die, as my parents went to church and I lay in bed. I remember feeling sick thinking about how they'd walk in there, and dad would shake hands with everyone, smile pleasantly and sing along to the hymns. How he'd tell everyone that, sadly, Blaze was home, sick with a cold.

Again. How often I was at home, 'sick'.

But that was one of the worse days, because Emma saw me in the state I was in. She was just twelve, I was fifteen. I was lying in my bed as still as possible because when I moved, my temples would throb with pain. There was a knock at the front door, not far from my room. I forced myself to get up and walk out to open it. When I did, I found myself blinking down at a wide eyed Emma, gazing up at me.

"Blaze?" she squeaked, as she took in my bandaged head with concerned blue eyes. "What happened?"

I ignored her question. "Aren't you supposed to be in church?"

"We left early. Daddy dropped me off so I could see you and give you this." She held out a small card, and on it were glitter glue words that said 'Get better soon'.

I took it and exhaled deeply. She'd never know that I wouldn't get better, not because of a stupid cold but of something much worse. Because of the deep ache inside. "Thanks. See you at school." I started closing the door. I wanted to get rid of her because I could feel the suppressed anger swelling inside of me again, and I didn't want to take it out on her.

"Wait," she stopped the door with her foot. "Don't you wanna hangout for a bit? And what happened to your head?"

"I fell off my bike," I lied. "And I'm sick. We can't hangout today."

Her body language said that she was hurt at my indifferent tone. She clasped her little hands to her chest. "Okay."

Instead of walking away, she just stood there, looking at me. Suddenly I was furious that she had to see me this way. Furious that she wouldn't just leave. I wasn't thinking straight, and before I knew it, I had shoved her back. She fell on the ground, a small gasp leaving her mouth.

"Blaze, I-"

But I'm already standing over her again. "Go away," I interrupt her. "You're a baby. You're only twelve. You don't understand anything."

When she still didn't move, I kicked her in her side. "Get up!"

She did, quickly, tears streaming down her face. She turned and started running away. Watching her speed off, I felt guilt twist my heart. Why did I have to go and hurt her? What was it in me that wanted to hurt an innocent and beautiful girl?

I felt I could throw up, so I did. I walked back inside to the bathroom and hurled.

I didn't have to worry about her saying a word to anyone. I knew she wouldn't.

Later that day, when I saw the car pulling up outside the garage and my dad's stormy expression as he slammed the driver's door, fear squeezed me. Mom must have said something wrong on the way home.

I knew what came next. Here we go again.

~ ~ ~

EMMA

My breath is coming out all funny, unevenly and jerkily. His fingers that are digging into my shoulders hurt. Where is Aiden? Why is he late? And why did Blaze have to come back early?

Looking into Blaze's eyes, I startle when I recognize what I see there. It's back. The burning fire of anger that resides in those hazel brown pools.

I flashback to when I still thought he was my hero.

It was a summer day in June. He was twelve, I was nine. We were playing hide and seek in the garden. I was overjoyed to be hiding with Blaze. I liked the feeling of being so close to him in our confined hiding space and I liked the sound of his breathing, in and out, in and out. I was safe with him and Carpenter wouldn't find us because we had the best hiding spot.

I wasn't expecting Blaze's hand to release mine and move up my arm, slowly. His warm touch against my own clammy skin tickled, and I let out an involuntary giggle, not knowing how else to respond. And Carpenter, who was passing by, heard it.

Blaze's hand abruptly slipped from my arm.

"Got you two." Eleven-year-old Carpenter's freckled face grinned as he peered around the bushes.

I felt Blaze stiffen next to me. "It was your fault, Emma. You shouldn't have made a sound."

I was sad at the disappointment in his voice. "Sorry."

"Aw c'mon, Blaze, it's just a game. No biggie. I'm going to go find the others." Carpenter said. Carpenter and Eddie adored Blaze. So did Patty. He was a 'big boy', older than all of us, experienced and wise. He always led us in every game we played.

As soon as Carpenter had left, there was a sudden, sharp jab to my ribs. It was enough to make a tear slip down my cheek. "What was that for?" I asked Blaze.

"For giving us away," he growled. Then he saw I was crying. "Don't cry, Emma, don't cry." He used his thumb to wipe the tear away. "You're too pretty to cry."

"B-but, y-y-you're angry with me."

"I'm not anymore, I promise. I'm sorry for hurting you, I won't do it again. Forgive me?"

I nodded and sniffed, glad to see him back to his normal self. I didn't know at the time how badly he was going to break his promise.

And I went back to believing he was my hero.

A rough shake of my shoulders brings me back to where I'm standing in the front yard, in front of my worst nightmare.

~ ~ ~

BLAZE

I regret everything I've done to her. Especially what I did that December night. But it's like there's something inside of me that I can't control, driving me on. A thirst to see that same panic that I felt in someone else's eyes.

Still holding her firmly, I spin her around and push her backwards until she's pressed against the door of my car.

She's looking down at her shoes again, or behind me, or above me. She refuses to focus on me.

"Look at me, Emma."

She doesn't. Pulling her forward, I throw her back against the car again, making her cry out. "Look at me now."

Slowly her chin raises and her eyes meet mine, vivid rings of shocking blue surrounding dilated pupils.

What happens next takes even me by surprise. I press my lips to hers and lean against her. She still has the softest lips, and her hair still smells of something sweet and citrusy at the same time. She struggles against me, trying to fight me off. I break away, but grab her wrists and pin them to the car.

"Go away. Leave me alone," she gasps. "I will tell my parents. I'll report you. I'm not afraid to. You will get arrested, like you were supposed to, almost four years ago." Her voice shakes with those last words.

I sneer, the monster inside of me taking control. "You won't. If you do, I will hurt you worse than you've ever been hurt before."

She fights to keep her expression stoic, but I can feel her body trembling. "You can't scare me anymore."

She doesn't believe I can win this battle? She might be thinking I'll hurt her physically, but I know other ways.

"Oh no?" I taunt. "I guess I should let you know I've been in town for a few days already. I've been watching you. Not only you, but..." I pause for effect, smiling down at her. "I see Patty has grown up to be very pretty. And bright. She likes spending time in the library, doesn't she?" Her eyes widen. "I should spend some time getting to know her, don't you think?"

I see the blood drain from her face and I know I've got her.

Author's note: So... *clears throat* Heavy stuff, huh.

I just have to say, quickly, that this is fiction. It has no real relevance (other then when I write about Jesus and God) to my life or to the lives of the people I know. Sure, I take stuff, little things and such from my own life and from observing others and from movies and books, but this is a work of fiction.

That aside, what did you think of this chapter? Too dark? And what do you think of Blaze's background? I know he has no right to treat Emma the way he does/did, but do you feel sympathy for him?

Lastly, you're awesome for reading thus far. I appreciate all votes and comments, they're like little gifts to me.

Chapter 16 - A Threat and a Mystery

Before December 31st

EMMA

I look at him and can't believe this is the same Blaze we adored when we were kids. Patty loved him. To hear him talk about her like this makes me sick to my stomach. My legs wobble and I feel desperate. I know exactly what he's implying, and I will not allow my sister to be at the mercy of Blaze's hands.

I take a sharp breath when he shakes me again. And then, swiftly, his grip is pulled off me and he's thrown back by someone else.

Carpenter.

My brother throws a punch at Blaze in a rage, but Blaze has more experience when it comes to this sort of thing and jabs back skilfully.

"Hey!" I scream, startling even myself at how high-pitched I sound.

Blaze stops first, and releases the hold he had on Carpenter's shirt. "Tell him, Em," he grins in a sickly way, his handsome face ruined by the ugly glint in his eye.

I feel shaky as I lie to Carpenter. "There's no problem here, Carp. Blaze and I were just...chatting. All is fine, really."

He scowls darkly at Blaze. "I don't think I believe that."

"Well, it's true." I assure him.

Blaze's eyes gleam at me with approval. He has me under his thumb. I step over on weak legs to stand next to Carp and give him a hug from the side. He looks confused.

"Are you sure, Emma?"

"Yes. Don't worry, I'm fine." I insist, smiling at my brother, trying to act like everything is okay.

Carpenter doesn't look fully convinced. He cuts his eyes at Blaze. "Stay far away from her in the future, or else I'm going straight to the authorities, after I beat you black and blue."

"Wow, I'm scared. Very scared." Sarcasm drips from Blaze's voice. "You heard the little lady. She said there are no worries, hakuna matata. And it's good to see you again too, buddy."

"I. Am. Not. Your. Buddy." Carpenter seethes, enunciating each word slowly.

I interrupt, seeing the storm in Carpenter's face. "It's okay. Okay? Just let Blaze take his stuff inside."

I hear the sound of Aiden's blue Jeep behind me. He's finally here. "I'll go now," I tell Carpenter. I know I wanted Aiden to meet everyone, but I can't stay any longer, not while he is here. "Bye, Carp." I pull him into another quick hug, then rush over to pick up my bags and make it to the Jeep before Aiden can get out.

I jump into the passenger's seat, slamming the door.

"Hey, blondie," Aiden greets me. "What's got you in a huff?"

"Nothing," I say, quickly, and try to replace my frown with a calm expression. But I can't help feeling slightly nauseous over what just happened. My sister is going to be staying in the same house as Blaze. It makes my stomach flip.

Aiden raises a brow. "Okay. And who's that?" he jerks his head in the direction of Blaze, who is unpacking his trunk.

"He's...our guest. Let's go, Aiden." I'm unable to stop the sense of urgency from entering my voice.

He gives me a worried glance, but starts the engine. "Sure."

~ ~ ~

AIDEN

From the way she's chewing her lip and barely listening to anything I'm saying, I know something is up with Emma. It's obvious she doesn't want to tell me though, so I let it go.

I'm still hoping that one day she'll trust me enough to tell me what she's holding back now.

On the way to Crystie's, a car overtakes us. There's a sticker on its dusty window with capital letters that spell out a bible verse. Or, at least I think it's from the bible, not that I have much knowledge of all that.

"For God so loved the world that He gave His only begotten Son, that whoever believes in Him should not perish but have eternal life." John 3:16.

I look over at Emma for a second and see that her brow is furrowed as she glares at the sticker. "I never knew God had a son," I say.

And what does it mean, that He gave Him? To us? How does that work?

She snorts derisively. "That's a load of bunny chow. Only unintelligent people will eat it up." Then her expression softens. "My family has fallen for it. Hook, line and sinker. They aren't dumb, though, they're just...fooled."

I smile a little at the term she used. Bunny chow. But I sober quickly. "So you know about all that...stuff? Like, Jesus stuff?"

Her glaze flits to me. "Yes, I know all about it. Had it drilled into my head since I was small enough to ride our Labrador."

Huh. I didn't know these things about her. Her family is religious? But I guess there's still a lot I don't know about her. "Do you go to church then?"

She shrugs. "Yeah. But that doesn't mean I'm a Christian."

"It doesn't?" I thought that going to church made you a Christian.

"No. Because I don't believe it in here." She presses a hand to her heart. "And I never will again."

There's a silence between us as I process that. What makes someone believe? What do you believe if you're a Christian, exactly? I want to ask her since she goes to church and everything, but something tells me she doesn't really like talking about it.

I'm way too curious to leave it alone now, though. I'll just have to ask someone else.

~ ~ ~

After dropping Emma off, I'm on my way to Garth's place when I see a familiar scene. In the neighbourhood park, Cleo lies on her stomach on the grass, a drawing pad in front of her.

I'll be late to see Garth, but something makes me park the car and get out to make my way over to her.

"Drawing again?" I ask.

She's so lost in her own world that my question makes her yelp with fright. "Wha...oh, hi Aiden. Um, yeah." She closes the pad quickly and gets up.

"You frighten easily."

"Well, I thought I was alone." She brushes herself off. "What brings you here?"

I lift and drop my shoulders in a shrug, suddenly a little embarrassed to be here just to see her. "Has that Daniel guy bothered you again?"

She blushes a little. It's cute. "No. Uh, about that. I want to say..." she rubs her left arm up and down. "Uh...thanks. For that. You know, for standing up for me."

I grin. "Anytime."

She offers a shy smile. Silence takes over, and there's no denying it's a little awkward. Then I say the first thing that comes to mind. "Can I see what you were drawing?"

Her eyes widen a bit. "Oh, I'm not very good. At all. I was just drawing a rough sketch and-" she stops midsentence when I bend over and pick up her drawing book.

"May I?"

She folds her arms. "Okay. Fine. But no laughing."

I open it and see a sketch of a little boy's face. It's beautiful. He has a freckle spattered nose and floppy hair. But what leaves me in awe is the eyes. They look so...real. "You're not good, huh?"

She shifts from foot to foot in a nervous manner. "Not really. I'm working on it, though."

"Cleo, you're right. You're not good." Her face falls a little and a smile tugs at my mouth as I tease her. "You're amazing."

She bites her bottom lip, holding back a smile. "Do you mean that? Like, you're not just trying to make me feel better?"

I shake my head. "You aren't blind, are you? Have you seen this stuff?"

I flip through the pages. There are still life sketches of flowers, more portrait sketches, and some landscape sketches of Stowe. I pause on the page that catches my full attention. It's of a man hanging on some sort of cross. He wears a crown of thorns and blood pours from his wounds. Below Cleo has written a verse.

The same verse I read earlier. John 3:16.

"Who's this?" I ask.

She walks closer to me and peers at the page. "That's Jesus. The Son of God."

I frown. "Why is he...dying?"

"Because He came to earth in fleshly form, to die for our sins."

That just makes me more confused. "Why would he have to die for us?"

"To pay the price for all the things we've done wrong. Because He loves us, He took our place and our punishment." Her face has taken on an almost unearthly glow; I can tell she loves Him. Whoever He is.

"I still don't understand." I say.

"It's difficult to explain...but I'd love to tell you about it. I'm still learning myself, but I can teach you what I know. Do you want to do that sometime?" Cleo suggests, her face hopeful after her rush of enthusiastic words.

Maybe she can help me understand what all...all this is, I think, as I look down at the man on the cross. Emma's face appears in my mind. She probably wouldn't want me delving into this. Hasn't she been there, done that, and rejected it?

Perhaps I'll find it's a load of garbage, like she said. But what's the harm in knowing that for myself? And if she doesn't know about this, it can't hurt her.

I nod slowly, looking into Cleo's brilliant green eyes. "I'd like that."

"Great!" Cleo exclaims eagerly and her green orbs light up. "I mean, cool. We can start next week?"

I smile. "Sure. But...Cleo?"

"Yeah?"

"Can you do one thing for me? Can you promise not to tell Emma? Or Garth, for that matter." I know Garth is far from being into the whole Christian thing.

Something I can't read shows up in her face for just a second, before it returns to normal. "I promise."

"Well, I better go. Garth is going to chew my ear off for making him wait." I hand the book back to her. Weirdly, I realize I want to keep it, but obviously I can't.

"Okay. See you around, I guess."

"Wait," I say, taking her book back and grabbing her pencil from where it sits behind her ear. "Can I write my number in here?"

"Yeah, go ahead."

I scribble it down quickly, give the book to her and then start walking away. "Bye, Cleo." She waves after me.

I stop halfway to the car. I don't understand the sudden gratitude I feel, but I can't ignore it. I run back to give her a hug. "Thank you," I say, as I wrap my arms around her and give her a light squeeze. She goes still for a moment, but then squeezes back.

"Anytime."

Author's note: So there it is. Chapter sixteen. As always, I am eager to hear your thoughts and opinion on this chapter! And you are the best for reading this. Thank you. The feedback and votes and encouragement I've been getting means so so so much to me.

I apologize for making you wait for an update...life got busy! It has a habit of doing that. But I hope that I will be able to post more regularly for a while now.

Happy reading, fabulous person. You can expect another chapter of this book to be up tomorrow!

Chapter 17 - Vandalism

Before December 31st

CLEO

I get home on Thursday after school. I had forgotten my phone before I left in the morning, so I check it as soon as I get to my room. There are three messages from Garth.

Garth: Hey Cleo. Wanna go for coffee at the Dutch Pancake café?

Garth: I can cycle to your house and we can go together.

Garth: Do you have a bike?

I saw Garth at lunch break but otherwise I haven't seen him today. He must have sent those messages right after school. I stifle a sigh. I thought I would be, but I'm not up to this. I have homework. And not only that, but I'll start thinking about Aiden or Daniel while I'm with Garth and I won't be able to concentrate on him.

I don't like letting him down, but it's probably for the best for both of us. I punch in my reply.

Me: Aw...I can't today...maybe during the weekend?

I send it and put my cell on the bedside table.

Daniel has ignored me since Monday. He must be mad at me. And Aiden...well, Aiden and I haven't arranged when we're going to get together to discuss the bible and all that's in it, but I'm excited for that. I get a goofy smile on my face whenever I think about it.

Lord, please may I be able to open Aiden's eyes with Your help. I know You want him to know You. So do I. And Daniel...

I really don't know how to fix things between Daniel and I. At the moment there's a lot I don't know. Somehow having Daniel suddenly reenter my life has changed the vibe between Aiden and I, in what way I'm not sure yet. I know that when I saw Aiden on Saturday, the butterflies that had swooped through my stomach before didn't happen. And I know they hate each other. I feel bad that it's mainly my fault.

I've kind of made a mess of things.

Well, Lord, please just talk to Daniel. Touch his heart in the way only You can.

Flopping onto my bed, I exhale heavily. I startle at the sound of my phone receiving a message. It's probably Garth. I roll onto my back and pick it up.

Daniel: Meet me at the Cactus Café in half an hour.

What. Daniel is messaging me?

When we were kids we used to meet up at the Cactus Café the whole time, especially during the holidays. It was our favourite hangout spot...and he remembers. I know it would be unfair and dishonest to say yes to Daniel now when I turned Garth down with excuses, so I decide that I have to say no. My heart sinks. I would have loved to catch up with him.

Wait, what? I scold myself mentally. Don't be disappointed. He was bossy and arrogant to assume he can just tell me when and where to meet him. And he was the one to completely end our friendship, a year ago. Should he really be allowed to pick up where he left off? Also there's the fact that the other day he was yelling at me abusively.

You're so sappy, I tell myself. He doesn't have any good intentions and he doesn't like you anymore, so get over it.

I want to reply with a mean message and act like I don't care at all, like I don't miss us and all we used to be when we were still friends. But as much as I'd like to act out, the truth is that I have forgiven him and I want to make things right between us. Not too long ago, I was holding a lot of bitterness in my heart towards him, and God convicted me of that, so I let it go. I forgave. I've been praying for him ever since. And I tried to ask Daniel to forgive me for the way I handled things and the decisions I made that may have hurt him. He must know that I tried, although he never answered my messages or calls.

It occurs to me that maybe I resent him a little for that now.

Jesus, help me to forgive as many times as I need to, the way You forgive me constantly.

I take a deep breath and let it go. I will forgive him, even if it's not seven times but seventy-seven. Because of the grace my God has for me, I will learn from Him how to love like Him.

Thank you, Lord. For giving me strength. For forgiving me.

I may not be able to have coffee with Daniel today, but I can take a rain check on that, surely. This could be the start of everything falling back into place, if we can just talk it over sometime and if I can convince him that things don't have to be the way they are.

Me: Can't today, sorry. Another time?

I only realize I was holding my breath for his reply when my phone pings again.

Daniel: Whatever.

Whatever? I'm surprised to feel tears pricking my eyes. He doesn't care.

Did I just lose my chance to prove that I do?

~ ~ ~

DANIEL

I don't know what made me message Cleo. I know I got my hopes up, though, and her reply was a low blow. She doesn't want to see me or be with me, that much is plain. I had a hunch that was true before, but it's been confirmed now.

She's probably with Aiden...

No. Shut up. What does it matter?

I just wanted to apologize properly for the other day. Maybe I don't need to, though, if she can't stand to be around me for just a little bit while I do. I should just push the whole thing out of my mind and forget about it.

I sit up and swing my legs over the side of the bed and start putting on my shoes. I need to get out of here. Out of my mom's dusty old apartment. Out of my small, cramped room where the only furnishings are a bed, a closet and a chair. Mom is working late. She usually does. Sometimes she only gets home at about one in the morning. I know because I hear her padding in through the thin walls, even when she's trying to be quiet so that I won't wake up. She doesn't know that I'm normally awake anyway. Then she pours herself some wine, takes of her shoes and switches the TV on. Often I find her sleeping on the couch early the next morning, and I have to gently shake her awake so she won't be late for work.

I stand, and stare at myself in the mirror on the wall for a moment. My nose is still faintly purple from Aiden's punch and the split in my bottom lip refuses to heal. Probably because I bite my lip without even realizing it. Turning away abruptly, I open the closet and grab my paint off the shelf. Stuffing the cans into my backpack, I tug my hood on and slam my bedroom door behind me.

In Boston, Massachusetts when I was staying with my dad, it was easy to get away with graffiti. All the kids I hung with did it. In dark alleys, behind old diners. Wherever. Here, in a small place like Stowe, it's going to be more difficult to not be seen. And vandalism is taken more seriously, too.

No matter. I'll be fine. Besides, I know I have to do this. It's the only other thing that gives me that feeling of escape, other than beating another kid up. Which I can't do, unless I want to get expelled a third time.

After leaving the block of apartments, I don't even notice that I am walking to Cleo's house until I'm almost there. It's like I never left, or like I have a map imprinted in my mind. My feet know the way there.

There's no one around the neighbourhood, the night air is dead with silence. I stand behind the two story house and look at my watch. It's almost midnight. Mom might be home soon, so I better hurry up and do this. I have to get home before she does so that I don't have to explain. Taking a few steps back, I take the red and yellow paint cans out of my bag and start spraying.

When I'm done, I stand and look at it for a little while. I grin slightly in satisfaction as I take in the display of glowing colours. She will know it was me, of that I'm sure. I've created something that only observant Cleo would recognize as my work. And I'm just as sure that she won't tell. She still believes in all that 'turn the other cheek' nonsense. My smile fades. Turn the other cheek and you'll walk away with a bloodied face, while the other kid leaves victorious. I've been in enough brawls to know that. But Cleo is so naïve and believing and gullible. The way I used to be.

Now I'm done with that stuff. God wants me to turn the other cheek? Well, where was God when my parents got divorced and I was so confused? When I was framed for something I didn't do the first time I got expelled? When dad told me he was diagnosed with terminal cancer and only has two years at most to live? And then after that, when I got expelled again and he told me he doesn't need me in his life right now?

Where was Cleo's big, mighty God in all of that?

I need to be in my dad's life right now. I'm the only person he's told about the cancer, and I want to be there with him. But I screwed up.

A memory comes to me as I start walking home. Me, on my bed, crying. My head in my hands. Cleo, sitting next to me, her soft arm stretched to wrap around the width of my shaking shoulders.

"It's okay," she's whispering. "God has a plan. You'll see."

A car honking brings me back to the present. The driver yells out of his window at me. I start running without looking back.

I almost believed Cleo back then, when she said everything would be okay. I prayed every day that God would change my parents' minds, that we'd be a happy family together once more.

But He didn't, and I stopped praying.

Author's note: And…chapter seventeen is finished. Hope you liked it. I, however, didn't feel too good about this chapter. If you can give me any advice, I'd appreciate it. I really want to know your true thoughts. :)

Also, here's something random. I love names and their meanings, and I have so much fun naming my characters. I thought you might enjoy the meanings for the names of the characters in this story, so I've put them below. Tell me what you think!

Aiden name meaning: Fire. (Celtic meaning) Do you think it fits well with his character or not?

Emma name meaning: Whole; complete. (English meaning) Which is a little ironic, 'cause she's a bit broken inside…

Cleopatra (Cleo) name meaning: Her father's fame; glory of her father. (Greek meaning) I like to think this name suits her, because she desires to bring glory to her heavenly Father.

Daniel name meaning: God is my judge. (Hebrew meaning) I just love the meaning and sound of this name.

Blaze name meaning: Lisp, stutter. (French meaning) Just thought I'd throw this one in as well.

Chapter 18 - Armour

Before December 31st

CLEO

It's Friday morning and I overslept after a late night.

"Mom's gonna kill you!" my little brother yells through the door.

"Cleo! You're going to be late for school." I hear the sound of my mom coming down the hallway.

"I'll be out in a minute, just hang on," I mumble, through the toothpaste and toothbrush in my mouth. I quickly put my hair up in a messy bun and then look into the bathroom mirror. I groan inwardly. It looks like a bird's nest, but I don't have time to change it now.

I finish brushing my teeth and grab my bag, exiting the bathroom in time to come face to face with mom. "Quickly! In the car," she orders.

We start down the passageway, my little brother and big brother on our heels. We half run to the garage and pile into the car. This is normal for my family, we're late for everything. As we pull out, something catches my attention. It catches everyone's attention, how could it not? On the wall of our house is a huge eagle, spray painted in red and yellow.

"What in the world?" my mom mutters. "Graffiti? In Stowe? And on our house, too?"

I gulp. There's no doubt in my mind who did this. And it's obvious he wanted me to know it was him.

~ ~ ~

During lunch I read the bible to calm my mind. I know Daniel must be angry with me, the eagle was an obvious enough sign. Although it can probably be easily painted over, it still worries me that he'd do that to someone else's property. How much did living in Boston change him? Something tells me the answer is drastically. I'm unsure of how I'll act around him now. Not that he's been near me much of late. I won't tell on him, because I don't think that will reach him. No, there's got to be another way I can make him let me in again.

I try to focus on what I'm reading instead of the noisy cafeteria surrounding me.

"For I am not ashamed of the gospel of Christ, for it is the power of God to salvation for everyone who believes, for the Jew first and also for the Greek." Romans 1:16.

Daniel once believed that the good news was true. With God's help and a lot of prayer, will I be able to help him believe that again? I want to see that light in his eyes once more.

Heavenly Father, I come before You and ask that You give me the words to say and guide all of my actions. I miss the Daniel that I know is still there. He's just hiding because of the hurt and pain of this world taking its toll on him. I know that You love him even more than I do and want him to be Yours again. Help me to be able to make a difference in his life for You-

-speak of the devil. I can't help that phrase popping into my mind in the middle of my thinking, even if it's no proper way to end a prayer, when Daniel plops down in the seat opposite me. I swallow.

Help me now, Lord.

Daniel frowns at my open bible. "Knew you were still into that garbage," he states, dismissively. I can tell it's on the tip of his tongue to call it something worse.

"It's not garbage," I say, firmly but calmly, even though inwardly I'm quivering with anger. "It's the Word of my Creator. And He's your Creator too."

He rolls his eyes sardonically. "Whatever."

Is that his new favourite word or something?

His expression changes from mocking to almost pleased when a slow, lazy smile creeps onto his face. I hate what it does to my stomach. Gosh, I've forgotten what a smile he has. Or maybe haven't. "Did you see the surprise I left you?" he asks.

The fluttering inside of me dissolves when I realize why he looks like the cat that got the cream. He knew all along that I wasn't going to tell. I purse my lips and remain silent.

He cuts to the chase, the smile slipping from his face when he suddenly leans forward, leaving only inches between us. I can see the scab on his lip from Monday's fight and the faint remnants of an ugly bruise on the bridge of his nose, but I ignore them when his vibrant light green eyes lock with mine. "Look, I know you're like an angel or whatever" -there was that whatever again- "but not everyone can be so perfect. You can stop judging, and maybe, if you want, I can teach you how to actually have fun sometime." He leans back and folds his arms defiantly, almost in a challenging way.

"If fun means vandalizing someone else's house, don't count me in," I snap, trying to shake the effect of having had him so close to me off. My words come out harsher than I intended them to.

He laughs. "You think graffiti is bad, little Cleo? You're in for a big surprise when you finally get a taste of the real world." I feel my face get hot at his patronizing term. This isn't the same Daniel that was defending me on Monday. "You have no idea," he adds, stressing the no.

You have no idea. The exact words he said to me before his fight with Aiden. There's something he wants to tell me, and there's something stopping him, I'm sure of it. "Then tell me, Daniel. Tell me what you've seen, where you've been. I want to know. A lot can happen in an entire year."

His eyes flicker and I know I'm right about him having something to tell. But he recovers the hardened glint in his glare all too quickly. He shakes his head and gets up to leave, but I stop him by placing a hand on his arm. He looks down at my pale fingers on top of his bronze forearm. "Daniel. I care. I never stopped caring about you."

His features remain solidly dull and unmoved. I don't know if he even heard me. Slowly, he takes my wrist and pulls my hand off him. He stands up to his full height, towering over me. A cold, denying smirk is his only reply before he leaves.

~ ~ ~

DANIEL

That was too close. I almost spilled everything. But I have learned by now that people only take what they want to from a story, and that they only listen to reply. Judging me is all I'd get in return if I had told her everything like I wanted to. If I told Cleo all of it, heck, even half of it, she'd hate me even more than she probably already does. Oh, I know she has the whole Christian 'I care about you and I'm here to help' thing down to an art. But underneath, no one really wants your problems to be their problem. Not even her. I'm too much of a realist to fall for that.

I may have known and trusted Cleo once before, but I have to be on my guard constantly now. I don't need any more complications in my life. And I surely don't need or want her 'help'.

Still, I can feel the light touch of her hand on my arm even now, as if it had never left. And I feel almost defeated knowing that I want to turn around and go back to her so that we can laugh and talk the way that we used to. But using every ounce of self-restraint I have, I force my legs to walk away.

I will not be defeated. Especially not by a girl who I thought I had finally left behind, in the past.

I most definitely have changed my mind about apologizing to her. It will only make her think she's winning. I've worked too long on crafting the armour I rely on; I won't let the emotions Cleo stirs in me tear it down.

But I'm getting tired of fighting by myself.

As soon as the thought surfaces, I push it away. Where did it even come from? Is Cleo already making me soft? I refuse to believe it. I may be a lot of things, but I'm not a sissy. It's just too many late nights talking- physical tiredness, that's all.

Then let Me fight for you.

I jerk my head up to try and find where the voice came from, but I'm alone, walking down the school hall. I shake my head at myself. I haven't been getting enough sleep.

~ ~ ~

AIDEN

Cleo has agreed to meet me at the library, on a Saturday again. A week later since I dared Garth and things have changed a lot.

I don't feel attracted to Cleo in the way I did before. Maybe I needed time to sort my feelings out, because I think I have answers that I didn't before. I know I'm finally ready to officially ask Emma to be my girl, and I have an idea of how to do it, too. But I am grateful to Cleo for taking time to help satisfy my curiosity about the bible and the man named Jesus...or at least, I hope she will be able to. And I'd still beat up Daniel if I saw him messing with her again. I feel a sort of fondness for Cleo, but no electricity.

Not like the spark I feel when I think of Emma.

Lately, Emma has been quiet and pensive. She was moody and otherwise when I went to the mall with her, Crystie and Crystie's brother, Bryan on Thursday.

When I asked her what was wrong, she just said, "Do you want there to be something wrong? Because there really isn't, and if you keep on asking I guess I'll just have to make something up so that you're happy."

I wasn't upset that she got mad with me. I was upset that she was lying to me. I could see it in her eyes.

She apologized later and tried to make it up to me by pretending to be happy, but it's easy enough to see through her façade when you pay as much attention to her as I do.

I have the suspicion that her gloominess has to do with whoever her family's guest is. I don't have a good feeling about him.

"Earth to Aiden." My little sister, Stevie, interrupts my train of thought. We're sitting at the table eating cereal in silence. Or, we were, but Stevie's rambling ruins it. "You weren't even listening! I was telling you about the play rehearsal we had at school yesterday. It went so well. You are coming to see the play, aren't you? It's in two weeks. It's called The Nutcracker. I'm going to be the Sugar Plum Fairy. You have to come, Aiden!"

Oh, but she can talk. "Of course I'm coming. Mom and dad would never give me an out anyways."

She frowns at me and pouts, one of her red curls falling over her face. I laugh at her grumpiness. "Don't worry. I want to come," I comfort her, meaning what I say.

Her face lights up again, and she takes a bite of her cereal. "Just wait till you see my dress! It's purple, like a plum purple, and so pretty." She speaks through her mouthful and I shake my head at her, smiling.

"Can't wait." I wink.

"Aiden!" I hear my mom calling as she walks into the room. "Didn't you say you had to be somewhere by ten?"

I look at my watch and jump up when I see the time, almost spilling my bowl of cereal in the process. It's quarter past ten already. "Shoot! I'm late!" I grab my jacket and backpack and dash out of the room, mom and Stevie blowing kisses after me.

Author's note: Heyyy people. I love you for your faithfulness in reading this story. Once again, feedback and votes are wanted and appreciated!Just wanted to say that my being vague about Cleo's family is not accidental. ..hold onto your hats, there's more to come surrounding that. Also, I have been suffering from a mildish case of writer's block. Pray for me! Haha, no, but really. I pray about my writing all the time.

Any tips, advice, and mistakes being pointed out are appreciated. Especially if you have an idea of how to make things more interesting in anyway...

Did you enjoy this chapter? What did you think about the fact that Aiden and Cleo are going to be spending more time together? How do you think Aiden is going to ask Emma to be his girl?

Chapter 19 - Questions

Before December 31st

CLEO

Aiden is late. I don't mind, though. I'm thoroughly enjoying reading Jane Eyre in the quietness of the library.

As I turn the page to chapter fourteen, a loud slam makes me drop the book. My head snaps up and I find myself looking at Blaze Brooke.

Not someone I want to see.

"How's school going, Cleopatra?" He bangs the table with his palms again just to make me jump.

Oh, I'd love to tell him to go away. To jump off a cliff. But I make myself stay civil. "Fine."

"Now, Queen Cleo, that's not much of an answer." I flinch at the old nickname. I haven't heard that since he left town.

He moves closer, and I watch him warily. "Since when do you spend time in a library?" I ask, trying to stall him.

"I'm full of surprises," he says, in a low tone.

Just then a phone rings. Blaze fumbles to retrieve it from his pocket and his expression changes after he answers it. Obviously, he doesn't like what he's hearing. He leaves as quickly as he came, holding the phone to his ear as he walks out. He shoots me a look that I read as to be continued before he does, but if he thinks he can scare me, he's wrong. I don't need to be afraid.

But I still send a quick prayer of thanks for the coincidental phone call.

Aiden enters soon after, looking a bit peeved. "Sorry I'm late," he says, as he sits down next to me.

"No problem."

"Do you know him?" he asks, and nods his head in the direction Blaze just went. They must have bumped into each other.

"Blaze? Yeah, I do." I pick up my bible and start flipping through the pages, hoping he'll leave it.

"How?"

"It's complicated," I smile apologetically, albeit tightly. This story is one I should leave for Emma to tell.

He frowns but doesn't press the matter.

~ ~ ~

AIDEN

So both Cleo and Emma know Blaze. Neither of them seem very fond of him at any rate. But my focus is returned to what I came here to do...ask questions, not about Blaze, but about Jesus.

Cleo already has her bible open. I peer at the page. The heading says 'The Gospel According to John'.

"So," Cleo starts. I notice she sounds a little nervous. "I'm normally the one being taught, at church and even at home, meaning I'm not used to trying to teach someone else. But I'll do my best."

I offer a nod. She looks a little flushed, but excited. "I appreciate it," I tell her.

She smiles. "If I'm honest, I'm not sure where to start. What do you want to know?"

I don't even have to think about my answer. "I want to know who Jesus is."

Cleo takes a breath. "I think...I think you'll only get to truly know Him by approaching Him yourself. He wants a personal relationship with you, Aiden. But what I am able to do is point you in the right direction, using this," she indicates the bible by tapping it lightly. "And I brought you one that you can study in your own time as well. I think you should start with John." She pulls out a book with a faded blue cover from her bag.

As I take it, I get the unbidden feeling that nothing will be the same after I read this book.

"I can tell you what I know Him to be. He is forgiving. He promises to protect us. And He loves us, unconditionally. There are verses in the bible confirming all of those truths. Can I read them to you?

I shrug, trying to feign nonchalance. Her eyebrow raises a notch and I'm not so sure I've fooled her. "Sure."

"1 John 1:9 says that 'If we confess our sins, He is faithful and just to forgive us our sins and to cleanse us from all unrighteousness'. He forgives you. All the things you've done wrong, any guilt and condemnation you feel...He can take it away."

I feel my chest puff a bit at this. "What is it exactly that I have done that's so bad?"

"I can't answer that, Aiden. But you can't tell me you've never hurt someone or lied or wronged another...can you?"

My head spins with that thought. I think about how I treated Adrianne a few weeks ago, for starters. Then, other memories come to me, lots of them. No, I can't say that. I let out a resigned sigh. "Guess not."

"Neither can I, trust me," Cleo grins slightly, and I relax.

She isn't scorning me and she isn't looking down on me. And I'm more interested than ever in what makes her different to everyone else.

A God that forgives. A God who protects. A God who loves.

Could He be real?

The rest of the morning passes by faster than I want it to. Cleo reads out verses and answers any questions the best she can. We laugh together now and then, share stories that relate to certain verses and I wonder at the shine in her eyes whenever she talks about Jesus again.

When I know I have to go so that I won't be late for my family's traditional Saturday lunch, she reminds me not to forget the bible. I want to tell her that I couldn't forget it if I tried, because I can't wait to read more as soon as I get home. I don't, though, for fear that she thinks I'm already willing to turn into a Christian or something.

I'm far from being ready to make that decision yet.

But anyway, the bible seems to be full of wisdom, whether I believe all of it or not.

Walking to my car that is parked nearby, I whistle and stick my hands into my pockets, causing dead leaves to crunch beneath my shoes as I go. The weather is beginning to get very chilly and I hunch my shoulders against the cold.

The sight of a blonde girl wearing just a t-shirt and jeans, her arms wrapped around herself and her lips blue from the chill in the air makes me stop.

Emma sits on a bench amongst the almost bare trees, leaves falling around her, staring into the distance. She doesn't even realize I'm there until I touch her arm.

She jerks back to reality from wherever she was. "Aiden!"

"You okay, blondie?" I ask, taking off my jacket and putting it around her.

"You don't have to do that, Aiden," she says, trying to push my hands away.

"Yes, I do. You're going to turn into an ice block if you just sit there in not nearly enough clothing for this kind of temperature. C'mon, I'm taking you home."

"No," she refuses, stubbornly, as she folds her arms.

"Emma. I will carry you again if I have to," I warn, trying to make her smile. She doesn't. "What are you doing here anyway?"

"I do my best thinking outside. I want to stay."

"Emma, please. You don't even have shoes on."

She just shakes her head mutely at my urging, and swings her bare feet as she sits.

"Does this have something to do with Blaze?" I blurt the question out before I manage to talk myself out of it. I know it was a bad idea when she stiffens at his name.

"Who's Blaze?" she pretends.

I suck in and exhale, making dragon breath as I blow out. "It's okay if you don't want to talk about it, but don't act like you don't know what I mean." I sit down next to her, putting my arm around her shoulders and pulling her closer.

Emma turns her face to me. "Your hair looks so red today," she murmurs, dreamily.

"And your face is white. You're going to get frostbite if you don't come with me."

"Don't you know of anyways to warm me while we stay right here?" she says mischievously, a half smile lightening her face.

I lean closer. "I might."

She laughs girlishly and looks down, her thick dark blonde lashes brushing her cheeks. I take her freezing hand in mine and move forward to plant a kiss on her lips. Without looking up, her other arm moves to hold the back of my neck. My hot breath mingles with hers as I share my warmth with her.

I pull away just as fast as I started the kiss, trying to ignore the strange but pleasant feeling in my stomach. Emma is shivering and I need to get her home.

"I really will pick you up again if you aren't cooperative," I threaten. I pull her by the hand to make her stand up. Her teeth are chattering.

"Promise me that next time you'll dress more warmly before deciding to do something like this?"

Emma just nods. She sticks like glue to my side as we walk to the car.

"Hey, do you want to meet my family?" I ask. "I was just heading home to have lunch with them."

"I'd like that," she says. She speaks softly, seeming distant and vulnerable. Pulling her even closer, I kiss the top of her head, smelling something sweet and citrusy.

~ ~ ~

EMMA

Aiden has an adorable redhead sister, Stevie, and an overly chatty but sweet mom. His dad is pretty quiet and actually reminds me of Aiden somewhat, but something tells me they aren't big chums. Still, I can feel the love as they tease each other over lunch. It makes me even more eager to introduce Aiden to my family, someday soon. Eddie is a year older than Stevie and I have a feeling they'd get on just fine.

"So, Emma," Mrs. Harper says, as she pours me more apple juice. "How long have you and your family lived in Stowe?"

"Well, I was born here. My parents moved here from Massachusetts when my older brother was one, and that was seventeen years ago."

Aiden's dad makes a hmm sound. "You've never lived outside of Stowe, then?"

I shake my head no.

"I don't miss Homestead much. It's much prettier here," Stevie says confidentially, picking a strawberry off the plate in the centre of the table. "And you're prettier than all of the other girls that Aiden ever liked."

I blush deeply at the sudden change of subject and unexpectedly having everyone's attention on me, as if they are observing me to see if it's true. I look to Aiden for help. He clears his throat, obviously a little embarrassed himself. "Can we be excused to go for a walk? Mom, dad?"

I admire the respect Aiden has for his parents. He hasn't back chatted them once or given them attitude. Before I can stop myself, I'm thinking of the contrast between him and Blaze when it comes to family.

"Emma?" Aiden's voice saves me from the direction my thoughts were headed in. "Wanna go?"

"Sure," I say, pushing my chair back and standing up. "Thank you very much for lunch, Mrs. Harper. And thank you for having me, Mr. Harper."

Aiden's mom smiles and her twinkly blue eyes look so much like his in that moment. "It's a pleasure, Emma. Feel welcome to call us Sara and Ben."

I smile back and then turn to Stevie. "I look forward to seeing you in the play, Sugar Plum Fairy."

She beams at me. The subject came up while we were eating and Aiden invited me to come with them when they go watch the play. It made me adore him a little more, that he would take time to watch his sister preform instead of hanging with his friends or doing something else.

Wait, you adore him? I almost grin at my own thoughts. Maybe I do, just a little bit.

As we walk in comfortable silence together, my mind wanders to earlier, when Aiden found me near the library. Momentarily I'm confused about why he was there in the first place, but that doesn't matter. What matters is that he was there when I needed him.

I have been feeling afraid lately, and the nightmares are worse than ever. I wake up thrashing and screaming, and Crystie has taken to sleeping next to me in my bed to comfort me.

But in the dreams, this time, it isn't me suffering from Blaze's blows. It's Patty.

"Penny for your thoughts?" Aiden asks.

"They're worth much more than that," I joke, although the truth is that they're too dangerous to share.

He grins. "Too true. But I'm kind of broke at the moment."

I smile before sighing and turning serious again. "Is it okay...if you give me time?"

He looks puzzled.

"I mean," I try to explain, "time before I tell you. I will tell you eventually, though, I promise."

Did I just say that? Haven't I got so used to hiding it away, and acting like nothing is wrong? Won't telling him just make it more real? I give myself as many reasons as possible, running through all of them in my mind, but at the end I find that I still want to tell him.

One day.

Aiden nods and links his arm with mine. I lean against his tall frame and savour this peaceful moment, tugging his jacket that he let me keep tighter and moving closer to his warmth in the cold autumn air.

He uses his fingers to play with my loose hair, his arm draped around my shoulder, and I let out a contented sigh.

Aiden makes thinking happy thoughts so much easier.

Author's note: Sorry this has been such a long time in coming...writer's block is no fun. Anyways, whaddya think? If you reckon you can predict anything in the future of this story, I just wanna ask that you don't share it with everyone else, so that they can still be surprised if possible ;) Don't want to sound all strict and bossy. Just asking nicely, haha.

Please go ahead and comment, vote, let me know your opinion, and all that.

I appreciate you.xxx

Chapter 20 - Milkshakes and a Decision

Before December 31st

AIDEN

After I take Emma home, I spend the rest of the afternoon alternating between finishing homework and watching television. I try to ignore how desperately I want to read the bible that Cleo gave me, because whenever I pick it up, I think of Emma. It almost feels like betrayal, after knowing how much she detests Christianity and all that comes with it.

That night, I can't take it anymore. If Emma doesn't find out, she won't have to worry about it. I practically jog upstairs in my haste to open and read the old, worn bible.

Before I know it, the more I read, the more I want to read.

Finally, at one-thirty the next morning, I get in bed. But sleep doesn't come so easily. Verses bounce off the walls of my mind, ringing out and resonating with something deep inside of me. One in particular refuses to leave me alone.

Ask, and it will be given to you; seek, and you will find; knock, and it will be opened to you. Matthew 7:7.

I want whatever it is that Cleo has. The joy that lives in her. The peace. Is it really true that all I have to do is ask? And then there's that purity about her. I find her freshness and innocence intriguing, in a way that makes me almost jealous of her. Another verse I read earlier comes to me.

Create in me a clean heart, O God, and renew a steadfast spirit in me. Psalm 51:10.

But who could possibly transform hearts or spirits? Surely it is not something that any being can control.

All things are possible with Me.

The almost audible voice makes me nearly fall out of bed. My heart beats fast and my palms sweat.

Who are you? I ask the voice.

I wait in deafening, time-stopping silence. And then the next words spoken shake me to my core.

I am the answer. I am what you have been chasing all this time.

The truth of His words makes me feel slightly weak. Realization hits me in full force and something else I can't name washes over me. Whatever it is, it feels great, despite my sudden light headedness.

For the first time in my life, I know I belong to Someone. Not to my parents, who have their own selfish ambitions and needs even though they love me. Not to the rest of the world, no longer do I have to be what they want to be. And most importantly, not to myself.

I belong to Someone much bigger and much stronger.

I suddenly have the urge to shout. Out my window, down the street, into the world. Tell anyone and everyone what just happened to me.

Then it comes to me, what I have to do. I was trying to keep all of this secret from Emma, but I can't anymore. I have to tell her. I have to show her what I have found. She can't have experienced what I have if she was able to walk away from it so easily.

But there's still time for that.

~ ~ ~

DANIEL

"Don't talk to me," I say, in a stony tone, as Cleo sits down opposite me.

I came to the Cactus Café to be alone. To sit in my regular place and place my regular order, then drink it and get out of here. I look down at my chocolate milkshake and can't help remembering how much Cleo dislikes chocolate milkshake. She would always pick strawberry. I wonder if she still does.

My unasked question is answered when a platinum blonde waitress walks on over. "What will it be today?" Her smile is almost too big for her face.

"A strawberry milkshake, please," Cleo smiles sweetly up at her.

After she leaves, I'm doing my best not to notice how soft Cleo's hair looks or how bright her eyes are today. I try to think about something else other than how she smells faintly of cinnamon or how her silver chain necklace lies perfectly in the groove of her collarbone. I gave that necklace to her for her fourteenth birthday.

"Something on your mind, Niel?" Cleo interrupts my distraction. Curse her ability to notice everything about me, even what lies underneath.

I wish she wouldn't use any familiar nickname on me, she probably has no idea what it makes me feel. A smile tugs at my mouth. I remember hers. Does she still get irritated when someone calls her by it? I decide to keep up my spell of silence and not test it out.

She sighs. "You always did win when we played the silent game."

I sip from my straw. Yes, I will be winning this one as well. If I just don't look at those wide, pleading, nearly forest green eyes...

Too late. I'm staring right into them.

~ ~ ~

CLEO

He has yellow and gold flecks in his amber green eyes.

Don't get lost in there, I tell myself. Just tell him what you came to tell him.

"Look," I start. "I wanted to say that...that...I...missed you."

Something unreadable crosses his face and then disappears. "Sure you did," he shakes his head and looks away. But I feel a slight sense of triumph at getting him to speak to me. Now just to keep him talking.

"Yes. I did. In fact, I still do." I play with the bracelet on my wrist, bracing myself for what I'm going to say next. I feel like a little kid again. "Daniel, can we be friends again?"

He laughs. He actually laughs. I let go of my bracelet, clenching and unclenching my fists beneath the table. The sound that used to warm my insides is now grating on my nerves, because it's laced with bitterness. "Don't you have other friends now? Aiden? That Garth guy?" he says.

I frown at what he's implying. And how does he know about Garth?

Instead of snapping at him like I want to, I compose myself and keep my voice steady. "Friends are a good thing, you know. The more the merrier."

Gripping the edge of the table so hard his knuckles turn white, Daniel turns dead serious as he grits his teeth at me. "Let's get one thing straight. I. Don't. Need. You. Any. More." He pauses in between each word to get his point across. "And I don't want to be your friend. Go care about someone else, because it's wasted on me."

His words sink like a sharp knife into me. "I want to help, Niel," I insist, tears burning my eyes.

"I don't need your help!" he snarls. "And you wouldn't be able to help even if I did. Don't think you've fooled me into thinking you have it in you to deal with the stuff I'm dealing with. Find another person who wants you to pretend you can help them."

He thinks I'm pretending? Can't he see that couldn't be further from the truth?

"I have made mistakes too, okay? I've been through the wringer before as well. You're not the only one." I do my very best to hold the tears back. "And you're so wrong, Daniel. I would never pretend with you."

He scoffs. "No, you wouldn't, would you. Neither would you crush me with a few words or never visit me in Massachusetts or think you're so much better than me."

My mouth drops open. "I told you. I don't fake around you. Would you have wanted me to fake feelings for you, Daniel? And I called, so many times. Maybe if you'd have picked up the phone I would have been able to arrange a trip to Boston." I take a quivery breath before continuing. "Also, never fool yourself into thinking that I see myself as better than you. Because I don't."

His eyes flash with anger. "Really? Well, you sure do a good job of acting like it."

"So you think I'm the world's greatest actor, huh?"

He shrugs. "Could be a new talent of yours."

I shake my head at him. "What did this to you? What made you how you are?"

Daniel's jaw tenses and I know I went too far. I hit a sore spot somehow. He stands up quickly, before fishing in his pocket and pulling out a ten-dollar bill. He chucks it onto the table. "That's for my milkshake. I'm leaving now."

I feel a sadness enter me as I watch him walk away. Again.

Lord, I did that all wrong. I don't want him slipping through my fingers this time. Show me how to reach him, please.

The cheery waitress from earlier drops by to plunk my milkshake on the table. I look at it with growing distaste. I doubt it will be enjoyable now.

She sees the expression on my face before I can hide it. "Aw, honey," she coos. "Was it that boy who made you look the way you do now?"

I read her nametag. Betty. "Well...he's just going through a bad time."

"I've got a bit of advice and you can leave or take it." Betty plants her hands on her hips. "Don't give up on anyone when they're going through a bad time. They'll come round in the end."

I smile. "Thanks. I don't plan to."

"Plan what?" Aiden is suddenly there beside her. "Hey, Cleo."

The waitress looks between us, gives me a wink and leaves.

"Hi, Aiden," I greet him. "Seems we keep on running into each other like this."

He grins. "Yeah. But I am really glad to see you. I have something to tell you."

I motion for him to sit in front of Daniel's half-finished milkshake. "What is it?"

He sits down, glancing at the milkshake. "You were with someone?"

"Yeah," is all I say. "What's got you so happy? The suspense is getting to me."

His smile grows bigger. He seems different somehow. I can't quite put my finger on it, but it could be-

"I made the decision," he announces.

I tilt my head to the right. "The decision?"

"Yes," his eyes shine. "Cleo, I'm a Christian."

Chapter 21 - Depth, Height, Speed

Before December 31st

AIDEN

Cleo's face breaks into a big smile. "You are?" she almost shrieks.

I nod. "Well, yeah. I mean, I think I am...I want to be. But I don't know if I did it properly?"

"Did you accept Jesus Christ as Lord and Saviour of your life and acknowledge that He is the Son of God?" she asks, her words tumbling out over each other, excitement bubbling up in each one.

"Yes," I say.

"Then we're now brother and sister in Christ!" Cleo exclaims. "Oh, Aiden, this is wonderful!"

I find myself grinning at her. "I feel so different."

"That's because you are! Hey, would you like to come to church with me sometime?"

I think about it for a moment. Yes, I would. "If that's okay with you."

She nods exuberantly. "Of course."

I feel eagerness rising up from deep inside of me. My whole life is altering, and I just know it's in a good way. I can't wait to tell Emma. It's new to me, but I'm already praying that she will hear what I have to say and that I will be able to convince her.

But first, I have a question I want to ask her.

~ ~ ~

EMMA

"Aiden, this is getting ridiculous." I squirm underneath his large hands that are placed over my eyes. "Where. Are. You taking me?"

"It wouldn't be a surprise if I told you, now would it?" he taunts. I can tell he's grinning at my impatience even though I can't see him.

"You won't have to worry about that. You never cease to surprise me." I say. I smile as well and we carry on walking on what seems to be gravel.

Blaze was full of surprises. Bad surprises. But this is different. I am only surprised in good ways when it comes to Aiden.

We come to a stop and Aiden puts his mouth close to my ear. "You can open your eyes," he says in a whisper that blows a strand of my hair forward.

"If you move your hands I might," I huff, pretending to be irritated, when in reality I'm tingling with anticipation.

"Okay, okay. One, two...three."

He removes his hands from my face and I blink. In front of me sits Mount Mansfield in all of its autumn glory. The sky is a bold purple-ish blue today and provides the perfectly aesthetic backdrop for the mountain that flaunts a thick covering of powdery white snow across its peaks. The wind whistles past me and raises goose bumps on my skin. It really is a beautiful day, even if it's been getting colder and colder lately.

I turn to Aiden. "It's gorgeous," I breathe.

His eyes sparkle. "Isn't it just? I love this place."

We stand a moment longer, taking in the rosy fall colours covering the mountain and the tall, proud trees. I move closer to Aiden for warmth in the crisp breeze and he puts an arm around me.

"Let's go," I say, excitement replacing wonder. "I can't wait to be at the top."

"Neither can I. But since I don't want you getting hurt again, I took the liberty of booking a cable car ride up."

I fold my arms and frown. "That was just once. I will be perfectly fine, Aiden."

He laughs. "Yeah, I'm sure you will, frowny face. But it's already kind of late, so if we want to get to the top and down again before it's dark, we should take the cable car."

I make a face. "Why are you usually right?"

"I think you meant to put always in place of usually there." He winks at me.

I roll my eyes. "You're impossible."

"And you're more beautiful than all of this," he spreads his hand, indicating the landscape in front of us, "even when you're mad."

I lift a brow. "I can't handle your cheesiness, you know."

"I know you like it." He beams at me and I disentangle myself from him to sock him in the shoulder, before walking off.

"Wait up, sunshine." Aiden is beside me again in two big strides of his long legs.

"Go away," I order. But we both know I don't mean it, and I can't help a smile from creeping onto my lips when he looks at me out of the corner of his eye.

Don't go away. Never leave me.

~ ~ ~

We stand on top of Mount Mansfield, the icy wind chilling me to the bone and making Aiden's cheeks rosy. Yet I hardly notice my shivers because of the picturesque spread that lies before us.

"Have I ever told you that," Aiden pauses midsentence and peers over the edge of the peak we stand on. "I'm afraid of heights?" He takes a few steps back and wobbles a little bit.

"What?" Worry fills me and I walk over to him. "Do you get vertigo? Do you want to go down?"

He shakes his head and takes my hand. "Nah. I shouldn't have said anything, never mind about it. It's not so bad. It's worth it to just be here with you."

More cheesiness. But he was right, again, when he said I like it. Does he really mean what he just said, though? He climbed Spruce Peak with me, even though that wasn't really high. And he took me for a ride in a hot air balloon. That was high. And now here on Mount Mansfield, he stands holding my hand as we look down at what you can safely call a very, very high drop.

He did it all for me?

"Are you just pulling my leg? Are you really afraid of heights?" I ask him.

Aiden shakes his head again. "I really am. But I have these stress pills that reduce my phobia slightly. I took some before we left. So don't worry."

I look up at him. I should probably get him off this mountain immediately, but I'm stuck in this moment. My heart is warm and happy because no one, especially not Blaze, has ever done something like this for me. "You're pretty cool, anyone ever tell you that?" I lean my head against his arm.

"Well...you aren't the first," he says, mischievously.

"Don't make me punch you again, mister big ego." I warn.

He chuckles. "Your punches feel like feather tickles."

I stand back a bit. "I'll show you feather tickles, buster." I roll up my sleeves and make fists out of my hands.

He laughs again, grabbing my wrists. His laugh is a wonderful sound that I wish I could record and play on repeat forever and ever.

All too soon his eyes turn serious. "Emma, I want to ask you something."

"Yeah?" I speak softly, wondering where this is headed.

He lets go of my hands and shuffles his feet, looking down for a moment and then lifting his eyes to meet mine again. "Will you, um...be..."

I elbow him. "Get on with it, you're making me nervous."

Aiden clears his throat. "Okay, okay, blondie. It's just that I've never done this before. But here goes. Will you, Emma Riley Rayburn, be my girlfriend?"

I let out the breath I had no idea I was holding.

There's only one word I'm thinking.

"Yes."

~ ~ ~

DANIEL

My phone has been blowing up with texts and calls from Cleo all day. She must feel bad about Sunday afternoon after the way things ended at the Cactus Café. I honestly don't care, I tell myself, as I rev my Harley and speed through town, colours and buildings melting into two blurs on either side of me. The bike was a gift from my dad when I first went to live with him last year. Maybe he thought it would start us out on the right foot.

Yeah, that didn't really happen.

Stop thinking about dad. Stop thinking about Cleo. You don't care anymore, remember? About any of that.

No one else cares, so why should I?

I care.

Those two words make me scared silly. I scrunch my brow into a deep frown as I stare through my helmet. Who is speaking to me? Mom told me when I was little that God often speaks to us like He spoke to Samuel, and that I should always be listening. But mom was wrong. It's just my muddled up head, making things up.

I start driving even faster, roaring past snack carts, little boutiques and pedestrians walking on the sidewalk.

Slow down.

Who's talking? I don't have to slow down if I don't want to.

Daniel, stop. Stop now.

I break hard, my heart thudding loudly against my chest. The screech of tyre against tar fills my ears. And then, the hysterical scream of a little girl.

I stopped just in time.

I jump off my bike, kick the stand into place and rush over to a middle aged brunette woman who huddles over her kid. Relief fills me when I see they are both alive and unharmed.

"I'm so sorry," I gasp, the adrenaline still rushing through my body. "I'm really, really sorry."

Slowly, the woman stands up, taking her little girl into her arms as she does. "It's okay, baby," she murmurs to the wide eyed child. Then she turns to me. "At least my Nellie is okay. But, boy, don't you ever go that fast again, you hear?"

Her calmness makes me calmer. "Yes ma'am."

They hurry off the road and the little girl waves at me over her mother's shoulder, as if I didn't just nearly kill her.

I get back on my bike and start it up again. "Thank you," I whisper.

I don't know who I'm thanking, not really. I refuse to believe it's God. If He's really there, why didn't He prove it when I needed Him most?

But I almost ran over a little girl. She would have died. She didn't.

Because I stopped.

No. I can lie to myself about this, but it will always haunt me. I was not going to slow down. I was doing what I've done so many times before, taking my anger and frustration and regret out on the road.

It was because something stopped me.

I have to tell someone about this. I have to talk to someone. And I know just who.

Author's note: Just two things I want to say today. Firstly, thank you for taking time to read this, I appreciate it more than words can say.

Secondly, I want to remind you that no matter what your future, past or present life looks like- God is in control. And He cares.

Chapter 22 - Sisters

After December 31st

AIDEN

Sometimes I wish I could go back and redo that whole year. Stop myself from messing things up and doing it all wrong. Other times I accept that what has happened has happened and that God has a much bigger plan.

I just can't see it yet. But I will, one day.

Still, it would be nice to be able to travel back in time and give my younger self some hard earned advice.

In the end, I guess I wouldn't have changed a thing, though, if it came down to it. Because that was the year I found what I had been looking for. A new hope, a new future, a new love. I found all of that in Jesus.

~ ~ ~

Before December 31st

CLEO

"You what?" I ask of Aiden, who stands in front of me as I put my books away in my locker.

I have been trying to concentrate on what he's saying, but it's a struggle, what with my mind relentlessly returning to the subject of Daniel. After ignoring so many of my calls and messages, he finally replied, asking me to meet him outside his mom's apartment tonight at nine. I'm as nervous as a cat about it, and have no idea why he wants to meet up with me now.

I guess I'll have to wait and see. I do my best to focus on my friend who stands right next to me now.

Lately, Aiden has been coming to me about all sorts of things. He's full of questions, and he also likes to talk about things that God reveals to him in his morning devotions. The other day he told me that he talked to his mom about all of it and that she wants to read the bible too. That bit of news made the whole day for me.

I have a feeling he's just told me something very important, and I could kick myself for not listening properly.

"I asked her out." Aiden repeats his sentence.

"You asked her...out? Who were you talking about again?" I close my locker and turn to face him full on.

"Emma. I thought you two were friends?" he says.

"Emma?" I squeak.

He nods, cocking his head to one side at my surprise. "She said yes."

Without meaning to, I put a hand to my forehead. Aiden eyes me, curious and confused. "Is that a bad thing?"

Yes. No. Yes. Of course yes.

I should have taught Aiden more about the bible. After all, I have had two weeks since he became a believer. And I didn't get around to covering one of the very important parts of the bible with him.

Do not be unequally yoked with unbelievers. For what fellowship has righteousness with lawlessness? And what communion has light with darkness? 2 Corinthians 6:14.

The verse is going around and around my head and Aiden is still waiting for my answer.

I know Emma better than anyone. I know that she is an unbeliever, even though she tries to hide it from me. I have been praying for her, every day and every night. She is damaged and jaded and she has turned her back on the God who only wants to help her. I've been begging Him to open her eyes. But she is stubborn and her heart is locked away.

I know all of this about her, and more. I know what Blaze did to her, I know about that December night. I know about the faint, faded scars on her wrists, because she showed them to me. I was the one who made her promise to never harm herself again.

I know how she loves Aiden already. I know that if he were to walk away from her, it would destroy her.

"Cleo?" Aiden's gentle voice bring me back from my thoughts. "You okay?"

I bite my lip. "Yeah...I just...I...do you know that Emma isn't a Christian?"

"Yeah. But I really think she's going to change her mind once I tell her what happened to me. I'm just waiting for the right time."

"She won't, Aiden. She will see this whole thing as you turning on her, betraying her. She absolutely hates Christianity." I hold up a hand to stop him from talking so that I can finish. "It might be different if it came from someone else, but from you...she thinks you're on her side."

Bewilderment fills Aiden's bright azure eyes. "What? What are you telling me? How do you know all of this about her, Cleo?"

"Because, I'm-" I stop short. I should have told him from the beginning. I brace myself to tell him now, and continue. "I'm her sister, Aiden."

He staggers back one step. "Her sister?" He raises his palms in a confused gesture. "You and Emma are sisters?"

I nod and duck my head, suddenly unable to verbalize the apology I had ready. Yeah, I should have told him.

Aiden frowns. "No, you're not. She only mentioned her once or twice, but Emma said her sister's name was Patty."

I lift my eyes skyward for a second. How I hate that nickname. It reminds me of burger patties, or the children's TV show Postman Pat, or the nursery rhyme Patty Cake. It took me forever to get Emma to stop calling me that at school and in front of other people, but I still let her when we're at home or when it's just us two.

"I am Patty, Aiden," I say. "My full name is Cleopatra. Emma took the 'pat' and turned it into Patty and has been calling me that since I was little."

Daniel used to call me that too, just to annoy me. I'd smile at the thought if this situation weren't the wrong time and place.

"Why didn't you tell me?" he scowls slightly.

"Because...I was afraid that as soon as you knew I was Em's sister, you wouldn't want to ask me anymore questions about the bible and being a Christian, for fear that she'd find out."

He shakes his head, almost like he's disappointed in me. "Then what about before I was even interested in the bible? Or after I became a believer?"

"It was just easier to not say anything about it, okay? I'm very sorry for not telling you. Forgive me?"

He just looks away and pulls his lips in a funny way, as if he's thinking. "Okay," he finally replies.

I chew my bottom lip again as I try to think of how to tell him what I need to tell him. "But the more important issue here," I say, "is you and Emma."

His eyes flicker to meet mine. "I still don't get why it's a bad thing, us being together."

I heave a sigh and put my hand on the back of my neck. "It's not bad. I mean, it is. Oh, it's so complicated." I move my hand to slide it down my face. When I look at Aiden, his stare is intense. He's waiting for an explanation. "Well, you've made Emma happier than she's been in ages, since...since Blaze." He frowns at Blaze's name. "And she's probably over the moon about you asking her. I have no idea why she hasn't told me, though, she normally tells me everything. She must not want me or my parents or brothers worrying about her after what happened to her in the past."

"What happened?" Aiden questions me. "And I still don't get why asking her out is a bad thing."

"I can't tell you what happened, only Emma can, once she wants to and if she wants to. But the point is, if you break things off with her now, she will never recover."

"Why would I? Cleo, you are really confusing me." Aiden shifts from leaning on his left foot to his right.

"Because. Because Christians aren't supposed to be in relationships with non-Christians. The bible says so, clearly."

His face changes as he processes this. "I should have first talked to her about God." He pinches the bridge of his nose with two fingers. "This is a mess. Are you saying I have to choose between Emma and God?"

I drop my head. I desperately don't want to see Emma get hurt again. But I don't want her to be the cause of Aiden going back on his newfound faith, either.

"Yes. That's what it comes down to."

~ ~ ~

AIDEN

I can't believe it. I care so very much about Emma. And from everything Cleo has told me, ending our relationship will put her in a bad place. But if it's true that it's wrong to even be in this relationship in the first place, then that's exactly what I have to do. Because I can't undo what has been done in me. I am a different person with different priorities. Jesus comes first. Even if I'm not entirely sure why I can't be with Emma, I will obey His word.

But I still have so many unanswered questions. What happened to Emma? Was it Blaze's fault? Just his name alone makes me see red. I knew he was trouble, since the day I saw him. And if he is the reason behind that untamed, lost look I see in Emma's eyes sometimes, then he'd be smart to stay away from me from now on. And why didn't Cleo just tell me they were sisters sooner? I suppose it is true that I would have not pursued my interest in Christianity if I thought Emma would find out. It's crazy that I never even suspected them being sisters, or had the opportunity to find out. Emma and I have been so caught up in getting to know each other and spending time together that I never even got to meet her family.

"Aiden?" Cleo looks up at me, worrying her bottom lip and on the verge of tears. "We both know what the right thing to do is," her voice cracks, "but I don't want to see Emma get hurt again."

I nod. I have no idea how I'm going to do this. One look at Cleo's upset face and I know she's in turmoil over it as well.

"She tried to kill herself before. She would kill me, too, if she knew I was telling you. But I need you to know how fragile she is."

Sorrow fills me at the thought of Emma trying something like that, and then anger. Whoever pushed her into the place where she resorted to such a thing is an absolute scoundrel. And I have a feeling that I know who it was.

I don't really know what to say, but I speak anyway. "I don't want to see her hurt, either, Cleo. But...I think you and I both know which choice I have to choose."

She nods and just barely suppresses a small sob. "I'm so glad that you're already all in for God, Aiden. Really, I am. It's incredible and it's definitely the work of the God I know. But it's just that I love Emma so much..."

I put a hand on her shoulder to let her know she doesn't have to say anything else. Just then, the school bell rings, making her jolt in surprise. We have to head to our classes now.

I watch Cleo for a moment longer as she looks anywhere but at me. She is clearly struggling with what is going to happen. She's one of those people who wear their every emotion on their face. And it's my fault that her sister is going to be hurting. I want to tell her that I'm going to have an open wound after this as well- an image of Emma's beautiful smile flashes through my mind along with the memory of her hand in mine and I know it's true. But more than that, I want to make it better. To go back and do it right.

But I can't make it better, not really, so I do the only thing I can. I give Cleo a tight hug and walk away just as the bell goes off again.

Author's note: So...they're sisters! Did anyone see that coming? And...thoughts? I know it was kind of long. A lot had to be explained.

Thank you guys for the comments and votes, advice and encouragement. :) Keep it coming!

Chapter 23 - Handcuffs and Consequences

Before December 31st

DANIEL

Through my smudged, dusty window pane, I see Cleo arrive. She wears a maroon beanie and a cream coloured scarf. The car that dropped her off leaves soon after she has gotten out. I wasn't expecting her to come, not really. Not after my last encounter with her and how I've been ignoring her.

But I'm glad she is here.

I leave my room to pound down the stairs to the first floor, grabbing my jacket on the way out. There's no doubt it's freezing outside.

I used to love summer, but I feel ready to embrace this coming winter, the already icy temperature when I walk outside singing in tune to something cold and hard deep inside of me.

As I walk along the sidewalk to where Cleo's petite figure clad in winter wear stands, looking up at the building of flats with her back turned to face me, I make up my mind to approach quietly. She has always scared easily, and the urge to creep up on her and give her a fright the way I used to when we were little kids is inviolable. Tiptoeing up to her, I hold my breath.

"Good evening!" I yell, grabbing her shoulders from behind.

She lets out a squeal, twirling around underneath my hands to face me, eyes big. When she sees who it is, she shoves me away. "Daniel, you dimwit!" she snaps, but it's so easy to tell that she doesn't mean it from the twinkle in her eye and the way she's trying not to giggle.

I find myself grinning, but force the childish smile to leave my lips when I do. For a second there I felt things were the way they used to be.

But that's dumb. It will never be the same and I shouldn't be allowing myself to be thinking like that. I let my hands fall away from her and I shove them into my pockets instead.

For what feels like an eternity, we stand looking at each other in the dim glow of a nearby streetlight, our breath clouding the space between us. I try to commit every detail of her face to memory, against my own will. I take in her features for the trillionth time in my life, but more slowly than I have before. Her thick, ebony lashes. Her almost heart shaped lips. Her button nose covered in little freckles. And the dark chestnut brown hair framing her pale face in waves.

Her eyes run over my face too, but not so much like she's observing, more like she's searching. Maybe she thinks there's still a little bit of the old me somewhere.

Too bad she'll be disappointed.

Cleo speaks up first, banishing the silence with her slightly husky voice. "So...why this? I mean, why did you want to see me?"

I think back to the other day when I almost ran over a little girl. "Because I needed someone to talk to."

She waits for me to go on, but I don't. She seems a bit anxious. I feel there's something else, too, an underlying sense of dread or distress. She's attacking her bottom lip with her teeth, something she would only do if something bad was going to happen when we were younger.

I tried so hard to forget Cleo, but apparently I still know her all too well.

"What's wrong?" I ask, breaking the second void of words between us.

"Nothing," she responds, far too quickly, as she absentmindedly tugs on a string of her hair. I don't feel the need to say anything else. I know her honesty will best her soon enough. "You're still able to tell when I..." she lets the rest of the sentence drift off.

I know what she means. Not that it's hard for one to see Cleo's emotions, but I am so familiar with the way she is that I can pick up even the most buried or hidden sentiments of hers. All of this time, I've been holding on, I've been remembering. And I hate myself for it. It will only cause me more pain.

Even though the alarms in my head are telling me not to care, I'm unable stop my next words from leaving my mouth. "If you won't tell me what's bothering you, then I won't tell you why I wanted to see you." I fold my arms and cock my head, waiting expectantly for an explanation.

She narrows her eyes at me. "You are not going to succeed in blackmailing me, Daniel Hayden Farley. I'm older now, you know. Not that gullible anymore."

I give her a smoulder of a smile. "We'll see about that, Patty Cake."

Her small hands form fists by her sides at the much hated childhood nickname. I turn on my heel and start ambling away, hands in my pockets again.

"Wait," I hear her call out.

I smirk. I knew I'd win.

"Come back."

~ ~ ~

CLEO

He turns and walks back to me, nonchalance in his every step. As he gets closer, I can't help thinking how I love the way his hair is visibly irritating him. It's long enough to tease his eyes when he blinks, and such a light golden brown that it's almost blond. Now and then he jerks his head or runs his hand through his hair in a vain attempt to stop the curls from getting in the way of his vision. He really needs to cut it. A smile plays out on my lips as a memory comes to me.

"Do you remember that day you wore a beanie to school in the middle of summer?" I ask Daniel.

He looks me up and down thoughtfully, as if deciding whether he wants to answer me or not. And then he does. "Who could forget the butt ugly haircut you gave me?"

The spark in his eye tells me he's missed teasing me. Well, I won't let him know that I've missed being teased.

"I'm so glad you gave up that dream of becoming a hairdresser," he adds, putting emphasis on the word so. "Think of how many people would be wearing beanies."

"Hey! You consented to it," I defend myself, "and you wouldn't stop fidgeting the whole time so it was mostly your fault anyways. But since I'm responsible and I own up to my mistakes, I'll offer my sincerest apologies and a voucher for a free haircut to make up for it."

He smiles a full on smile. Not a smirk, or a taunting grin, but a proper, real smile. "That's much too generous of you, Cleo, considering your incredible skill in the art of hair is much sought after. I regret, I cannot accept."

"Are you positively sure?" I give him a slow, sly smile. "It would be no problem. I could even do it now."

"No," he says hastily, feigning an expression of horror, "thank you."

I try not to laugh out loud. Somehow that would be a little too much like old times, and I'm not sure if either of us are ready for that yet. But I'm hoping against hope that we're getting closer to it.

I still have the photo we took of him the day of the haircut. It really was hideous, so I don't blame him if he isn't eager to be anywhere near me when I have a pair of scissors at hand. I stifle another chortle that threatens to escape me.

"Okay then." I pout and keep my eyes downcast as I drag my right foot in circles on the pavement, pretending to be offended and trying to prolong the light hearted mood.

No such luck. In two strides he's inches away from me. He uses his index finger to tip my chin up. I meet his questioning gaze, his face serious now. "What's up, Cleo?"

I know what he's talking about. I thought I had made him forget the question he asked earlier. Not so fast, apparently. I won't get away from him, so I guess I'll just have to answer him.

"It's about Emma," I say, keeping it vague.

His eyes soften. I wasn't supposed to, but when we were thirteen, I told him the whole story. He knows all about it.

Daniel opens his mouth to say something, but he never gets there, because another voice pierces the still night air with a yell. "You there!"

A man dressed in black from his boots to the cap on his head charges out from the shadows towards us and before I know it, he's grabbed Daniel and pulled him away from me. The badge on the man's shoulder and the instruments hanging from his belt give away his identity as a Stowe patrolman.

I wonder what Daniel has done now?

"What's going on?" I voice my thoughts, as Daniel scowls severely at the man and struggles to get away. But he's a big guy, and he's already cuffing Daniel's wrists.

"I'll have you know who you're keeping company with, young lady. A scoundrel bent on ruining the peaceful neighbourhoods of Stowe." The officer finishes securing Daniel's hands. "Stop fighting me, or else I might be convinced to use my taser. Your 'artwork' around town has not been appreciated, and finally I have tracked you down."

Oh great. The graffiti. I should have known. He was obviously going to leave his mark on other places in town other than my house.

"Officer..." I start.

"Scott Kirkpatrick," he supplies, in a gruff tone that warns he won't be taking no nonsense.

"Officer Kirkpatrick," I continue, "Please consider letting my friend go just for tonight. I will make sure he throws away his paints and never gives you cause to come looking for him again...ever." I cut my eyes at Daniel and he rolls his own in response.

"I'm sorry I can't do that, missy," Kirkpatrick almost growls, not sounding sorry at all. "He has done enough to convince my superiors and myself that a trip to the police station is what he needs."

I suck in a breath. No, although Daniel may deserve this, it's not what he needs. I already know things can't be good between him and his dad for him to have moved back to Stowe, and his mom might not be too impressed with him either after this. If I can just get him out of it somehow and then keep him away from more trouble after that, instead of letting him go with the police officer now, it will allow my mind to rest easier. Something tells me neither of those will be easy to do.

I try to think fast because Kirkpatrick is already attempting to tow Daniel, who is making it hard, away with him.

"Stop!" I shout.

The irritated patrolman stops and huffs at me. "Give me one good reason why, girlie."

Girlie? Yuck. But I have a bigger problem. Why should he stop?

"B-b-because." My words tremble. "It wasn't him," the white lie slips from my lips. I'm cringing inwardly and my insides are turning. I haven't lied in so long, and I'm already asking for forgiveness from God for what I'm about to say next. "I did it."

The police officer looks me square in the eye. "You did it?"

I nod, gulping silently. The dishonest statement I uttered is already twisting my conscience, but I need to do this for Daniel.

"Then explain to me, girlie," Kirkpatrick squints at me menacingly and gives Daniel a shake to keep him still. "why I was able to track this ruffian here down because of a witness' sketch. They were very adamant that it was a tall young man, not a girl."

The way he spits girl out of his mouth makes me mad.

Daniel has stayed silent throughout all of this, but now he gives me a what in the world are you doing kind of look. I need to come up with a good answer, and quick, or else there's no way I'll be believed. "I, um, he, he needed the money, so I paid him to do it."

Oh, well done, Cleo. You paid him to do it? Is that it? No, you are a really bad liar, is what.

Scott Kirkpatrick looks confused now. "You paid him to do it?" he frowns. "Well, I suppose that makes you an accomplice, although I've no idea what the point of paying someone to vandalize for you is. I guess both of you will being coming with me tonight, then."

He lunges forward and grabs my arm, his fingers digging deep into my flesh. I choke on any more words I was going to say to try and fix this. Daniel still hasn't talked, but I see his jaw muscle clench as I give a small yelp when the policeman's hand squeezes me even tighter. Then, in one swift movement, Daniel elbows the policeman in the stomach and kicks his shin. The man doubles over for a second, manages to keep his grip on Daniel, but lets me go in the process.

Run. Daniel mouths at me.

I turn on my heel to do just that, but I don't get very far because a big black boot slides in front of my right foot and trips me. I put my hands in front of me to try and block my fall some. My action assists in getting away with only scrape on my cheek as I hit the ground with my palms and then roll to the side, but my left wrist already aches with a sharp pain.

Kirkpatrick, with his right hand still clutching Daniel's handcuffed hands, yanks me up by my sore wrist. I let out a shriek of pain and his hold on me gentles a little, but it still hurts like crazy.

This is not going the way it was supposed to.

Chapter 24 - Bad Memories

Before December 31st

And before the arrest of Daniel and Cleo

AIDEN

It's crazy how October has flown by. It will be November tomorrow, marking it as two months since I met Emma. Stevie's play is at the end of November. I wonder how on earth I'd be able to still take Emma to the play after I end things between us and not feel like it's supposed to be a date? Maybe I won't have to, maybe she won't want to see me. Yeah, she probably won't want to see me. But my heart is already hurting at the thought of that. She has become more than someone I'm attracted too, more than someone I like. She is my best friend.

And now, as I drive to the Rayburns' house, on time at seven o'clock for the dinner I was invited to, my gut wrenches at the thought of what I have to say to Emma, eventually.

Not long after Cleo and I had our serious conversation earlier today, Emma found me at school and told me her parents want to meet me.

"You must come for dinner tonight, Aiden," Emma had said, tugging on my arm, eyes shining. "My parents will love you, and you'll finally be able to meet my brothers and sister. And our guest is staying at one of his friends for the night. I won't be taking no for an answer."

It's most probably a good thing Blaze wouldn't be there, because I had feeling I'd find it difficult to be civil.

Looking down at her glowing face and those baby blue eyes I loved so much, I could not bring myself to tell her we can't be together anymore. Later, I told myself, as I accepted her invite. There's time still.

I'm still telling myself that now, as I walk up the steps to the Rayburn household's front door. I will meet Emma's family, and I'm positive I'll like them. I'll have a good time talking to everyone during dinner and being with Emma, and I'll do my best to not think about what will follow in the days to come when I'll have to finally find the courage and guts to break both our hearts.

I tell myself all of this, then I take a deep breath and press the doorbell.

A boy about thirteen or so opens the door and grins widely at me. He must be Eddie. His face looks familiar and it takes me a second to realize it's because it was his portrait that I saw sketched in Cleo's drawing book once. His floppy light blond hair reminds me of Emma and his sparkly green eyes are a tell-tale sign of his relation to Cleo.

"Hello," I greet him. "Eddie, right?"

"Yup. Edward Rayburn at your service," he responds playfully, before looking me up and down quickly. "And you're Aiden." It's a statement, not a question. "You're even taller than she said you were," he adds.

I laugh. "How old are you, Eddie?"

"Almost fourteen," he replies.

"You're kind of tall for your age yourself, you know."

His smile grows bigger. "Yeah, everyone says so."

"Eddie!" a familiar voice calls out. "Can you please stop pestering our guest and actually ask him inside?"

Emma appears beside her little brother, looking like a dream with a lovely beam on her face and her hair in an elegant bun, soft tendrils escaping to tickle the sides of her face. She ruffles Eddie's hair and he scowls at her.

"I see you've met the baby of the family," she says.

I grin at them both when Eddie's frown deepens. "Baby? I'm already almost taller than you," he retorts.

"But still young inside," Emma pokes his chest and giggles at his expression of annoyance.

It makes me feel a little more at home already. Stevie and I tease each other all of the time, sometimes it's the only kind of love a sibling knows how to show.

A slightly distant, deep voice takes me away from my thoughts. "Aiden," Emma opens the door wider and makes space for the person who has walked up next to her. "Meet Carpenter. Carpenter, meet Aiden."

I shake his hand. Not quite as tall as me, but quite broad shouldered and a little grumpy looking, he sizes me up with suspicion in his eyes. My guess is that he's very protective. "I've heard a lot about you."

Carpenter raises a brow, but seems to relax a little at my friendly tone. "If I know Em, it's probably not all that good," he jokes.

I shake my head. "Actually, I don't know what she's let you think, but I've got to admit that to me it sounds like she adores you."

"Is that so?" he turns to Emma, wrapping an arm around her shoulders. "Well, little sis, you know I'll be holding you to that from now on."

Emma gives me a look that accuses of me of being a traitor. I laugh.

"Well, are we gonna go eat or what?" Eddie asks. "I'm starved."

"Eddie," Emma gives him a disapproving glance, before rolling her eyes in fake exasperation and focusing on me again. "These brothers of mine never stop eating, it's like they have bottomless pits for stomachs."

"Sounds familiar." I pat my own stomach lightly. She laughs, and I feel a sort of magic in the air when she does. I'd never get tired of hearing that laugh. But pretty soon I know I might have to learn how to live without it.

Don't think about that.

As we all walk inside, Cleo appears in the hall. I wonder if I'm supposed to act like I haven't met her yet or not.

"Aiden, good to see you again!" she gives me a quick hug and steps back again.

I take my cue from her. "Hey Cleo."

Emma looks at me, confused. "You know each other?"

"Yeah, we, uh, met recently." It's true. I only met Patty today, even if I met Cleo a while ago.

"Em," Cleo says, angrily, but we can all tell she's just playing. "How could you have told him that my name was Patty? I'm going to get you back for that. I thought my days of being Patty were finally over."

"Oh, you will always be Patty to me," Emma taunts, and Cleo shakes her head.

"Hi there." A middle aged, petite woman whose face looks a lot like an older version of Emma's enters the hallway. It's getting crowded in here, but I like these people so much already that I don't really care. The woman who I assume to be Emma's mom gives me a smile, her eyes doing exactly what Emma's do when she smiles, crinkling at the corners. "Emma hasn't stopped talking about you today. I'm glad to finally meet you, young man."

"And I'm thrilled to meet you as well, ma'am." I say.

"It's just Marlene. Or Marli, if you like. Welcome to our home! It's so good to have you here. Shall we head to the kitchen? I'd appreciate some help setting the table, kids."

We all move into the kitchen and just after we finish laying the table together, I hear the sound of the front door opening. Mr. Rayburn must be home. I tense a little. I definitely want to be able to give the truthful impression that I only care for his daughter and wouldn't harm her, ever. He walks into the room soon after, and proceeds to give his wife a kiss and his daughters hugs and his sons slaps on their backs before turning his attention to me. I realize after a beat of silence that he's waiting for me to speak first.

"Mr. Rayburn, I'm Aiden Harper." I reach for his hand. "It's a pleasure to meet you."

He nods. He has the same dark hair as Cleo, I notice. "The name is Trent. And I can say the same. It's good to finally meet you. Emma's rather good at keeping secrets, but I am glad she thought you were one worth sharing." He gives Emma a glance before he lets go of my hand. It's easy to tell he's both protective and fond of her. "So, people," he claps his hands together. "Let's eat!"

~ ~ ~

After dinner and a dessert of s'mores that everyone had fun making and messing on themselves, Emma and I walk out onto the porch to sit on the swing bench there.

We sit without speaking, but it feels right. Her hand reaches for mine and I hold tightly, trying to warm her freezing fingers.

I sense she's about to say something, but whatever it is, it doesn't come in time before Cleo bursts out of the front door. "I'm going to be late," she says, wrapping a scarf around her neck. "Carpenter! Come on!" she yells back into the house.

"Coming!" comes the muffled reply from Carpenter.

"Are you sure you want to go? He hasn't given you a reason to want to see him again," Emma tells her. I look between the two of them, trying to figure out what's going on.

"Emma, it's Daniel. I've known him almost my whole life. I need to go see him, to see if it's possible we can make things right again."

"Okay." Emma gets up to give Cleo a hug and whispers something in her ear. Seeing them next to each other, I realize where I've seen this scene before. On my computer, when I was first infatuated with Emma and I was stalking her on Facebook. Cleo is the girl who was standing next to her in those photos.

Carpenter chooses that moment to show up. "Okay, Cleo, I'm ready."

They leave, Carpenter to drive Cleo wherever she's going to see Daniel, and Cleo to go see him. I don't have a great feeling about Cleo going to see that guy after what I saw between them when I first met him, but I know I'm not in charge of her.

Emma comes to sit down beside me and picks up my hand again. We talk for long, maybe an hour, about lots of different things. I use my fingers to follow the patterns on the palm of her hand as I hold it. Carpenter comes back in that time without Cleo and winks at us before going inside the house again, but I have a feeling he'll be keeping an eye on us from somewhere.

After a while there's a lull in our conversation. The quietness between us is comfortable, but I'm still wondering what it was she was going to say before we were interrupted by Cleo.

I don't have to wonder long. "Aiden...there's something I should probably talk to you about." I wait. This is it, I guess. The time for her to tell me what happened with Blaze way back when. But by the look on her face, she's not finding it easy. "It's about Blaze, but maybe you know that already. We used to be really close. I thought I was in love, even at such a young age and...I didn't see who he really was. I realize that his father wasn't the best of dads, and the effect it had on Blaze wasn't a good one. I didn't know that, though, until after he-" she swallows and stops talking.

I trace a circle on the knuckles of her hand to try and soothe her. She'll continue once she's ready.

"I-I trusted him, you see. We were just kids. Young and dumb. But I trusted him." She goes quiet again.

I already feel sorrow for whatever it is she has yet to tell me. And anger for Blaze rises within me. I clench the hand that isn't holding Emma's.

~ ~ ~

EMMA

It's much more difficult to talk about it to Aiden than I thought it would be. I want him to know, but I have to think for a while about the words I'm going to use.

My mind flashes back to the December when I was almost thirteen years old. More specifically, to the last night of that December.

We were having a barbeque with Blaze's family. While the food was on the grill and the adults were talking, Blaze and I were wandering around the garden looking for something to do.

"Hey, Em," Blaze said.

"Yeah?"

"Wanna go for a walk around the neighbourhood, just the two of us?"

I had felt a swarm of butterflies enter my stomach. Blaze wanted to be alone with me. Could this be time for my first kiss? My parents would disapprove, I knew, but Blaze was special. It would be special.

So we went for the walk.

I can't even remember what I said that angered him, but the next thing I do remember is him knocking me to the ground behind some shrubbery, throwing his foot into my side, my arm, my thighs. I was whimpering, afraid to scream in case it made someone come and Blaze was even angrier at me for it.

Then he did give me my first kiss, but not in the way I imagined it. No. With tears streaming down my face in rivers and as I tried to push him away, he kissed me. As if it would make it better.

I squeeze my eyes shut at the memory of what comes next.

I let out the breath I had been holding captive, and like plunging mindlessly into icy water in the middle of water, I launch into the full story of how Blaze took something from me that didn't belong to him. And how I know it's my own fault for being so trusting and naïve.

When I'm done, tears are slipping silently from my eyes. But I feel better.

Aiden puts an arm around me and draws me closer. His body feels tense. "Aiden? Are you upset?" I ask, my voice coming out hoarse because of my crying.

"Very," he grinds out. "If I ever see him around it's going to take a lot to hold back from beating him till he's dead. Emma, no young girl, no girl, no woman should have to go through something like that because of someone like him."

"Aiden, that isn't why I told you. It's in the past, okay? But I just wanted to show you...that...that I trust you. Because I don't think you're like him. Am I right in trusting you?" I have to know. Blaze didn't keep his promises, but Aiden has so far.

I shift my head to look into his eyes. I see something unreadable and unfamiliar in them before it quickly disappears. "Emma, I can promise that as long as I'm around, I won't ever do anything like that to you or allow anyone else to, either."

I nod. But something is nagging at me. He didn't say yes.

He loosens up for my sake and wraps both arms around me securely as I lay my head against his chest. I could fall asleep right here. "So I can trust you?" I repeat in a murmur, sleepiness starting to take over my body.

I feel the rumble in him when he clears his throat. I wait patiently for his answer, but it never comes, because there's a sudden commotion inside the house that we can hear from out here. We both get up in a hurry and go inside to find out what the noise is all about.

I almost run into Carpenter. "It's Cleo," he says. "She's been arrested."

Chapter 25 - Someone To Talk To

Before December 31st

DANIEL

The clock on the wall reads eleven pm.

Cleo and I sit handcuffed in Chief Donald Hull's office. There's dried blood on the side of Cleo's face and a nasty bruise surrounding it, but it doesn't look so bad compared to her swollen, blue wrist. We sit in silence, me fuming over the fact that no one has bothered to send a medic for Cleo's injuries, even if they aren't major, and Cleo looking a little dazed. Loud voices outside the door alert me to the probability that her parents have arrived. I know that my mom won't be here, since she's most likely only going to be done working at twelve or one in the morning. I glance at Cleo again. I know her being here is my fault, even if she did go and lie to a police officer, earning herself a ride to the police station with me. That surprised me, I have to admit. But it isn't as surprising as the feeling that is settling in now. Gratitude. Something I haven't felt in a long time. She did something she didn't have to do for me, to try and help me.

I swallow, tapping my right foot against the floor and allowing my eyes to wander back to Cleo every few seconds.

Just say it. Get it over and done with.

I sigh. Here goes. "Cleo."

Her head turns to me and she waits for me to carry on. She looks like a bit like sleepy kitten, her hair all rumpled and her eyes droopy.

Stop stalling and stop thinking about how cute she is.

Wait. Cute? Shut up, I order myself, wishing I could slap my forehead with my palm to knock those stupid thoughts out of my head. But obviously, the cuffs are preventing that.

"Thank you," I finally say.

I had thought Cleo was in a dreamy mood, but her eyes clear a little and a smile graces her face. Oh, no. I recognize that smile. It's her smug smile. So much for grace. "Did Daniel Hayden Farley just thank me for something?" she grins teasingly at me.

"Whatever," I mumble.

She laughs before composing herself seriously again. "Anytime, Niel."

I don't reply. Instead I look away, rolling my shoulders forward and then back in an attempt to get rid of some of the stiffness in them, as well as trying to ignore that I'm uncomfortable knowing how she made me feel warmer inside with the words she just spoke.

"Daniel?"

I shift my gaze to her once more. "Yeah?"

"I kept my end of the bargain. Now it's your turn to tell me what's going on." Cleo's expression is one of forbearance and calmness. Something tells me she won't let this get away easily.

Why does she have to be so darn persistent? Well, if she really has to know, I'll let her know. I'll give it to her straight and then watch how she takes it. "Okay, fine. The other day I almost ran over and killed a five-year-old girl. My grades are bad. My mom barely eats, she just drinks, and she's working so many late nights that it's wearing her out. And, to top it off, my dad has cancer and the last words he said to me before I left Boston were to tell me that he can't stand being near me anymore. He wants to spend the last year of his life in peace. Without me." I don't expect my voice to break, but with the last two words of my explanation, it does.

I wait for her eyes to fill with pity, or a kind of disregard, or a reflection of what she must really be thinking: that I'm a loser of a son and that I deserve being sent away.

But that doesn't happen. All I see in them is compassion.

"Daniel, I had no idea," she whispers, sparkly tears threatening to spill from her enchanting green orbs. Her lip quivers a little. "I'm so sorry."

What I would really like to do is cross the room and hug her, not that it would be easy while I'm wearing these handcuffs, and cry with her. But I don't, because I'm not a little boy, and even if she's pathetic, it doesn't mean I have to be. I grimace at her. "Yeah, well, that's life, Cleo. Newsflash. Or maybe you'll only find that out someday, when you finally open your eyes." Ouch. Even I wince inside at how gruff my tone is.

"Daniel, I...your dad-"

I cut her off. "Don't. Don't worry your pretty little head about it."

"But..." she's struggling to keep the tears at bay, I can tell.

"I told you," I snap. "I told you what you wanted to know. Isn't that enough? Can you leave me alone now?"

She straightens up in her chair suddenly, wiping each eye with the sleeves of her joined hands. "I will not leave you alone, ever. As long as you're in Stowe, you're going to have to put up with me, following you around, asking you questions, talking to you. You know why? Because, Daniel, you were my best friend. I still care about you, even if it's not mutual anymore. I still want to be there for you. So deal with it. You can't expect me to get over nine years of friendship, just like that. It's not happening. I won't let you go the way I tried to last year. I failed miserably anyway." Cleo takes a shuddery breath and stops.

I'm stunned into silence with her speech and the authoritative tone I don't hear often when it comes to Cleo. But the cat doesn't keep my tongue captive for long. "Guess I'll just have to get a restraining order, huh. I can do that tonight, I suppose. I'll just tell chief Hull that there's this weird girl who is threatening to follow me everywhere."

She glares at me. "Not funny."

I laugh and she sighs. "Can you at least accept a truce?" she asks.

"Hmm...that depends. Will you buy me lunch every day for two weeks?" I give her an angelic smile.

"Daniel!"

"Okay," I'd raise my palms if I could. "A truce it is."

Somehow, letting out the whole truth to Cleo has made me feel lighter, like a space inside of me was filled with led and now it's gone. But still, I feel empty. Like something else needs to fill that space.

Me. Let Me in.

"Stop it!" I yell, and try to place my hands over my ears, before I realize I can't. Because, of course, they're cuffed.

"Daniel?" Cleo looks at me with concern. "You okay? You gave me a fright."

I can't tell her. She'll think she knows exactly who is talking to me, and I won't believe for a minute that it's her 'powerful' God. "Yeah. It's just...there's a strange ringing in my head," I lie.

"Oh." She frowns. "Well, I hope it goes away."

I shrug.

Cleo is way too sweet. And she was wrong about what she said earlier tonight- she's still very gullible.

~ ~ ~

CLEO

I watch Daniel curiously. He's moving his foot against the carpeted floor, hitting it relentlessly with the toe of his worn out sneaker, and I wonder if he even notices.

Lord, I pray, if there's anything You want me to say to him, give me the words to speak.

I'm still a little shocked at his revelation. I can't believe that Zach Farley, the fun loving, bear hugging man I remember, has cancer. Or that Kathie, Daniel's sweet, gentle mom, is an alcoholic.

Pray with him. The voice I've come to know so well urges me.

"Would you like to pray with me?" I suggest to Daniel. His head jerks up and he looks at me as if to say, of course not.

He shakes his head a little vehemently. "I'm not going to pray. But, I won't stop you, if it makes you feel better."

"Fine," I say. "Then I'll just pray by myself." I breathe in, out, ask again for the right words, and start. "Lord Jesus, I thank You for all that you have done for both Daniel and I. Thank you for the things You have provided us with, food and clothing, enough finances to get good educations. I pray now for Daniel's schoolwork, please give him wisdom, understanding and perseverance. I pray for Kathie, that you give her peace and rest. And I pray for Zach, that you will heal him completely of the cancer in his body. I thank You that You love us all. In Your wonderful name I pray, amen."

Daniel's head went from hanging to snapping up sometime during my prayer. He murmurs an 'amen' and I don't know if it's out of habit from years past or if he means it. I realize it's the latter when he looks at me, eyes intense and the yellow flecks in them almost glowing. "Do you really believe He can heal my dad?"

Mark chapter ten verse twenty-seven comes to my mind.But Jesus looked at them and said, "With men it is impossible, but not with God; for with God, all things are possible."

I nod, holding his stare, excitement tingling my insides because he just referred to God like He exists, instead of acting like He's a fairy-tale the way he has been doing recently. "I do believe that."

Just then, the door bursts open. "Cleo!" my father booms.

Uh oh.

Author's note: So. Sorry this chapter was kind of short.If I'm honest, I'm unsure of how well this story is going. My thoughts are...well, not so well. But I'm praying about it and I'm persevering.

Thank you for reading! If you have time, I'd really appreciate you leaving a comment for me to read later.

xxx

PS: Who is your favourite character? (Out of the main four)

Chapter 26 - Early Hope and Early Snow

Before December 31st

DANIEL

Somehow, Cleo's dad manages to convince the officers to drop the citizens' charges and their own against me. I don't know how, but he does. It's only on account of me getting rid of my paints and promising to never vandalize any properties in Stowe again, though. If I do it one more time, they won't be very forgiving.

I'm feeling overwhelmed. Not so much because I spent half a night in the police station, but because twice in twenty-four hours, two different people did something unexpected and kind for me. First, it was Cleo, who tried to get me out of trouble, and then her dad, who cleared things up with the law for me.

Don't get me wrong, he's still mad as anything.

"Do you realize what you got my daughter into tonight, Farley?" he says, tersely, as he drives us both home. I want to hear him call me Daniel, but I know what he must be thinking about me now.

I nod. Then, realizing that he obviously can't see me from his seat in the front because he has his eyes on the road, I clear my throat. "Yes, sir."

"You're lucky Kirkpatrick knows me and believed us about Cleo not being involved." I can see from the backseat that he's frowning severely, by the reflection in the rear view mirror. "First, you disappear from her life when she thought you were her best friend, never answering her attempts to reconnect and causing her more hurt than a man ever wants to see his daughter take. And now, this."

I find myself accepting his words. Honestly, I feel like I deserve them.

Wait, what's happening to you? Cleo is as much at fault as you are over how things happened. Don't get all mushy about it now, I tell myself.

I bite the inside of my cheek and decide to ignore his stormy remark instead of defending myself, and flash back to when Trent Rayburn was more of a father to me than my own distracted, busy and hardworking dad.

Things have changed, for sure. Not the part about my dad being busy with other things, but rather the fact that Mr. Rayburn is not very fond of me anymore.

Cleo sits next to him silently, her hands folded in her lap. Her wrist still looks bad. I was glad when her dad got all up in Kirkpatrick's face about it.

"And you, young lady," he gives a quick glance to Cleo that speaks volumes of his disappointment and fury. "I really thought I could trust you not to lie to an officer of the law. At the very least, I thought you would be smart enough not to."

She opens her mouth as if to say something, and then wisely closes it again, ducking her head. She is indeed smart if she knows not to make any retorts when Trent Rayburn is in a huff like this. We drive the rest of the way to my apartment in soundlessness that I would normally find peaceful, but everyone is too on edge for that to be a possibility. I'm angry at the same time I'm thankful towards both Cleo and her dad. And I'm mad at myself, too, for getting myself into a situation like this again.

I feel something else as well, something other than frustration or vexation. Something much worse, something I haven't experienced in a long time.

Hope.

Ever since Cleo's prayer for my dad, I've been wondering. Is it possible? Could God heal him? Would He heal him? Does He even exist, after all?

I try to swallow my hopefulness, willing it to land in the pit of my stomach so that I can do my best to forget about it. Feeling this way just leaves too much room for a huge let down, and even though I'm familiar with disappointment, I'm not particularly partial to it.

~ ~ ~

CLEO

I don't care that I'll probably be grounded for months. I don't care that my face hurts from the fall, or that I have a balloon wrist. All the way to the stop where we drop off Daniel, I'm praying that God will work on his heart. Maybe good will come out of our arrest, if I'm remembering the look in his eyes when I prayed for his dad's healing as clear as it felt then. It's like something had come alive inside of him.

"Out, Farley." The car jerks to a stop, and I come to the realization that my dad just ordered Daniel out.

"Dad," I mutter.

"What?" He turns to glare at me.

"You don't have to be rude."

Dad sighs and runs a hand through his hair, his expression softening. For the first time, I notice the few threads of grey streaking through his brunette thatch. "I'm sorry, young man," he addresses Daniel, who is getting out of the car without a word. "But you have to understand that this is not what I want for Cleo. You are welcome to come for dinner sometime, and you are still welcome in our house. However, I forbid you and her to spend any more time alone together. At school, I want you to stay away from her. The same goes to you, Cleo. After tonight, I think it's wise that there be always be a chaperone when it comes to you two."

I can't believe he no longer trusts me.

Wait, scratch that, I can believe it. It's not like I've been on model behaviour mode tonight. But still, can't he understand I was just trying to help? And that Daniel is not a danger to me? How will I reach my best friend that I know is still in there somewhere if I can't talk to him?

Daniel still hasn't said anything.

"Do you understand, Daniel?" my father asks, gently. That's the first time he's called him Daniel, and if I know my dad, it's a sign he feels bad.

Daniel nods. "Thank you both for helping tonight." He speaks low, so that my ears barely catch his sentence. He closes the door quickly and we drive away.

~ ~ ~

EMMA

The week after the night I tell Aiden what I've hidden from everyone else is a blur. Cleo is grounded, and miserable. She won't talk much about what happened that night, but I don't mind. I know how it feels to not want to tell anyone. Instead of prying, I try to make her laugh whenever the opportunity comes around. I long to see her enthusiasm come back and that sweet smile return.

Since I talked to Aiden about Blaze, a weight has been lifted from my back, like I'm more free now. And even though I've only seen him in passing lately, at the cafeteria, in class, on the school grounds, I feel closer than ever to Aiden. He texts me constantly and every time, he manages to make me feel a little happier inside. I'm daring to believe he still likes me the way I am, even after the truth of what happened to me has been revealed, and after I kept him in the dark for so long.

To make things even better, I haven't run into Blaze again, not once. Living at Crystie's has been fun, and mom says that Blaze will be leaving town soon anyway, since his mom's funeral is over.

I sit with Crystie now, on the couch in the lounge, snuggled up with blankets and hot chocolate. The winter weather is fast approaching, just a few more weeks and it will be December. To think that this December will be so much brighter than all the others since Blaze, because Aiden will be here with me, definitely puts me in the holiday spirit.

"Let's put the Christmas tree up today," I suggest to Crystie, just as Bryan walks in to the room.

"Are we having a snuggle evening? Awesome," Bryan all but jumps onto the sofa next to Crystie, yanking some blanket over himself and grabbing her hot chocolate.

"Hey!" she squeals. "Give that back, Bryan."

He smiles a goofy smile and hands it back, but not before taking a sip. "Mmm."

Crystie slaps him and roughly ruffles his shaggy brown hair, but she's giggling. "You're lucky you don't have this dork as a twin brother," she tells me. I laugh at them.

Bryan snorts and rolls his eyes. "Did you say something about a Christmas tree, Em?" he wonders, changing the subject.

"Yeah. I was thinking we could put it up today."

"Sounds great," he rubs his hands together. "I've got dibs on putting the star at the top."

I fake a scowl. "No fair!"

Crystie laughs. "You two are such kids."

"Hey, I'm younger than you, Crys, I get to be immature," Bryan replies.

"You're younger by one minute." She shoots him a sardonic look.

My phone rings, making us all jump. "You have the ugliest ringtone I have ever heard," Bryan comments, and I shush him with a frown and a finger to my mouth as I answer.

Okay, so it might be a lame ringtone...it's the theme song from Barnie. But honestly, I don't care what anyone thinks about it. I used to watch that show as a little kid, and it's a tiny shrapnel of what my innocence used to look like. Before Blaze took that innocence and shattered it.

"Hello?" I speak into the phone, even though I know who it is.

"Hey blondie," Aiden says. "What are you up to on this fine Saturday evening?"

I smile. "Lazing around. Not much."

"Sounds nice. Listen, I have to talk to you about something." His tone is suddenly serious and urgent. I don't like it.

"Sure," I say. "We're drinking hot chocolate and putting up the Christmas tree at Crystie's place. Want to join us?"

I wait a few beats for his answer. He must be thinking. "Okay, I'll be over soon," he finally says.

~ ~ ~

I giggle as Aiden and Bryan fight over the star. "I called dibs!" Bryan yells. "Tell him, Em, I called dibs, didn't I?"

I make an innocent expression and bat my eyelashes. "I won't pick sides."

We're all high on hot chocolate and marshmallows. Crystie lies on the couch, covered in tinsel. Aiden and Bryan play wrestle each other for the golden star. I'm watching them out of the corner of my eye while I hang the other finishing decorations on the tree. Eventually, Bryan wins, and he proudly stands on tiptoes to reach the top of the rather tall Christmas tree. Aiden huffs and crosses his arms, pretending to be disappointed.

"Awh," I coo, taking his arm and squeezing it. I can't help noticing it's bulky with muscle, and then blushing at my own observation. "Next time, Ade."

His brows lift. "Ade?"

I shrug. "Do you like it?"

He grins. "Yep. First nickname I've ever received. I like it."

I beam up at him.

"Yuk. Lovebird alert." Bryan quirks his eyebrows and makes a face.

I blush again when I see Crystie is looking at us too. "Whatever this is," she says in a teasing voice, "please take it outside."

We all laugh and I throw a bauble at her, which she dodges.

"I should get going anyways," Aiden announces. "It's kind of late."

I nod. "I'll walk you out then."

I throw one glance behind me, just in time to see Bryan grinning and Crystie winking at me. Losers. I'll get them for this.

"Bye, you two!" they chorus.

We walk away, my hand in the crook of Aiden's arm. It's already dark outside. No sooner are we out the door, when something cold and tiny lands on the tip of my nose.

A snowflake.

I squeal in delight. "Aiden, it's snowing!"

He looks to the night sky. "It is indeed." He reaches out to catch another snowflake in his hand. "This is the first time I've ever seen snow."

I look at him. "I love snow."

Aiden smiles. "Then I'm sure I will, too."

When we get to his car, I ask the question that has been on the tip of my tongue the entire evening. "What was it you wanted to talk to me about?"

He looks down at me. His expression is a strange one, like he's weighing different options in his head. "You know what, it's nothing really," he finally responds. "I just wanted an excuse to see you."

A smile tugs at my lips and I look down at my boots. When I lift my eyes again, he's looking at me with a look so intense it makes my heart beat quicker. My gaze is locked with his. Slowly, he leans forward, until our foreheads are pressed together and both our eyes are closed. Then he moves again, capturing my lips with his. Instinctively, I reach up and put my arms around his neck, and he wraps his around my waist tightly, as the kiss deepens.

All too soon, it's over. He pulls away gently, looking shy all of a sudden. My lips still tingle with electricity and I don't let go of my grip on him. The snow is falling around and on us in flurries now, melting into my clothing and piercing my skin.

"I don't want to," he says hoarsely, "but I have to go."

I bob my head and move back a space. He leans in to give me a quick, soft touch of his lips on my cheek, before he gets in the car.

~ ~ ~

After December 31st

AIDEN

I should have talked to her like I was going to that evening. But I didn't.

And I'm reminded of it every day since.

Chapter 27 - A Miracle

Before December 31st

DANIEL

Two weeks after I'm released from the Stowe Police Station and banned from going anywhere near Cleo, I lie in my bed on a Sunday morning, trying to go back to sleep so that I can avoid an awkward and one sided conversation with my hungover mom who is probably in the kitchen attempting to make pancakes, if my nose is right about the smell. Conversing with her would be one sided because I have spent too much time away from her and I don't know how to act normal around her anymore. She chatters away to fill the silence I allow, and now and then I simply say 'yes' or 'no' or 'I don't know', until she eventually gives up. Kathryn Farley used to be a stable, happy stay at home mom who baked the best banana bread. Or at least, that's what I remember. The divorce changed a lot of things.

From my room, I hear the doorbell ring. I slide my pillow out from underneath my head and hold it against my face. Mom will get the door. I hope. But after it rings three more times, I have no choice but to assume that mom either can't hear it or has fallen asleep again. The apartment suddenly smells like burnt pancakes, and I then know it's the latter.

Jumping out of bed, I open and rush through the door of my room dressed in only tracksuit pants and a pair of socks. First, I run into the kitchen to turn off the hotplate beneath the burning pancake that sits in a frying pan. Mom sits at the counter on a stool, her head on her arms, fast asleep. I curse under my breath when I burn myself on the pan as I put it in the sink. I leave quietly, so as not to wake her. As soon as I'm out, I jog to the front door, opening it and coming face to face, inches away from the person who waits there.

Not who I expected to see.

Cleo stands in front of me, shyly averting her eyes from my bare chest, her hands clasped. Noticing her discomfort, I hold up a finger. "One second." I dash to my room, pull on a shirt and I'm back in front of Cleo in no time. "Why are you here, Patty? I thought we weren't allowed to see each other."

"Well..." she begins. That's when I realize there's someone else just behind her.

My dad.

"Hello, Dan."

He's always called me Dan.

I tense and nod. "Hi, dad." I shoot a questioning look to Cleo.

"Uh, my dad said I could give Mr. Farley directions, because he didn't know that Mrs. Farley, uh, I mean, Miss Kathie had moved here. He wanted to see you," she explains nervously, and moves aside for my dad to come in. "I'll be waiting downstairs," she tells my dad, and he smiles at her before closing the door.

"Quite a special girl you've got there. Don't let her go again," dad says.

My cheeks flame. "She isn't and never was and probably never will be my girl, dad. I don't have the choice of letting her go."

He shrugs. "I think you're wrong. I saw the way she looked at you, and you at her."

I shake my head angrily, and turn away. "Are you forgetting that she has already told me that she doesn't feel that way? Or were you not listening to me when I told you, as usual?"

I immediately regret what I've said when a look of hurt flashes across his face. It seems to me that there are new wrinkles since I last saw him, around his eyes and lips. His salt and pepper hair has even thinned a little more. Or maybe my eyes are playing tricks on me. But it would make sense, since cancer lives in him and is slowly eating what life he has left inside of his body.

"Son, I'm sorry for the way things ended the last time we spoke. Please forgive me for everything I said. I wasn't thinking clearly and I take it all back. There's no one other than you that I'd rather spend time with. I realize that now."

I still, whatever defence I had ready dissolving. I just said ugly, hurtful words to my dad who is already in enough pain, and he's apologizing to me? "Yes, dad, of course. I forgive you. And I'm sorry for what I said, I didn't mean it."

He doesn't speak, but pulls me into a hug. My dad is at least six-foot-tall, and I almost get a fright when I realize I'm taller than him now. By nearly an inch. Time is passing so quickly, and I don't want it to.

When we stand back, his green eyes, the eyes everyone says are the very reflection of my own, are solemn. "I have to tell you something."

I nod for him to go on.

"Dan, the other day," he pauses and swallows, suddenly seeming to be overcome with emotion. "The other day, I went to Dr. Harrison for treatment. After some tests and an examination, he gave me the greatest news of my life. Dan, I'm cancer free."

I take a step back. It's like something slammed into my chest, hard. I feel like a feather could knock me over. "Cancer free?" I echo.

"Yes! Yes. Can you believe this? It's a miracle. Never have I believed something like this could happen, until today. I'm healed, son!" My dad is grinning like a little boy, and I think he'd be jumping up and down if he weren't the dignified, cultured adult that he is.

I furrow my brows. "No way," I breathe.

"Oh, but, yes way," he claps his hands excitedly. "I want you to come live with me again. I have missed you so much. But we can talk about that later, right now I've got to get to church. I'm taking Cleo and we're going to the church we used to go to."

My head is still spinning. I can't believe it. I won't believe it. It's impossible.

"All things are possible with God," he tells me, as if he was able read my mind. "I'm so sorry that I've doubted Him for a long time and allowed you to doubt Him as well. But, I've seen it for myself- no, experienced it for myself. He is able! Please tell me you'll consider coming to church with us this morning?"

"B-but," I stammer, searching for the right words. I can't go to church. God won't want me after I've denied Him so many times, and shamelessly, too. "But what about mom? I have to take care of her. She isn't feeling well," I lie. Well, actually, it might be true, with a hangover like the one she has.

My dad's expression falls, before turning concerned. I know he still wants mom to be okay, even now, after everything that happened. "Tell her I hope she gets better soon, okay? And if either of you need help with anything while I'm in town, just call me." He grips my shoulders with his hands and squeezes. "And Dan? Don't forget what happened. I'm healed, and it's thanks to our Saviour. I know God will settle that in your heart in time."

I say nothing. If He really did do this and He really does exist, He'll want nothing to do with me now.

"Now, don't want to make Cleo late. You think about what God has done for us. It's truly wonderful." His hands slide from my shoulders and he starts for the door.

"Okay."

"Okay," he repeats. But he doesn't make a move, just stands there.

"Can I ask you something?" I wonder aloud.

"Sure."

"Why didn't you just call me and ask for directions instead of bringing Cleo?" My face heats with shame at the realization that she must have seen what a mess this place is.

Dad lifts and drops his shoulders. "I wanted it to be a surprise."

I smile to encourage him. He suddenly looks a bit sad. "It was an awesome surprise, dad. But you're going to be late...remember?"

He startles. "Oh, yes, oh yes. I have to go, then. Bye, Dan, I'll see you soon, for sure. Not missing a chance to catch up with you."

After he's gone, I go to the kitchen and pick up mom to carry her to her bed. She's so light and skinny, it worries me. Too much drinking and not enough eating. I tuck her in and stare down at her pale, yet peaceful face for a moment. Padding out of her room softly, I close the door and turn to rest my head against it.

The full shock of what I've done comes to me.

Cleo prayed to God and my dad was healed, and I have denied the God who does exist. I won't be worthy of recieving His love now, or His help, or the strength that He gives to those who love Him. I won't have His friendship. As a little boy, whenever things went wrong, I would pray and feel so much better. His presence was always there, holding me together, all along. How come I am only realizing that now?

There's no place for me with Him anymore. It's too late.

No, it isn't. My arms are wide open. Come to Me now.

The hairs on the back of my neck stand up and goose bumps cover my body. I finally recognize that voice.

I get to my room as fast as possible, almost knocking a frame off the wall of the hall in the process. I quickly peel off my clothes and spray deodorant on. I have no time to shower. I get dressed in clean clothes and stumble out on the things strewn across the floor of my messy room. I write a note and place it by mom's bed, along with a glass of water for when she wakes up. I grab my keys and waste no time in locking the apartment door after me and thundering down the flight of stairs to get to my bike.

I'm going to church.

~ ~ ~

CLEO

My heart sinks when Daniel doesn't exit the building with his dad. Does he still not believe, even after this?

Lord, please show Him truth. Like You say in Your word in John: *And you shall know the truth, and the truth shall set you free.* Set him free, Jesus. Only You can do that.

"You ready to go, Cleo?" Mr. Farley asks. He looks disheartened himself.

"Yes," I reply. "Let's go."

We drive to church, making small talk on the way. He asks how school is, how my family is doing. Since I told him about the episode in the police station and how I prayed and Daniel agreed, he's been thanking me. Thanking me for praying for him and believing for him when he didn't believe. I'm thrilled to see this revival in his heart, but I have to constantly remind him that it had nothing to do with me, and that all the glory goes to the One who did the healing.

It is amazing, what He has done.

"So, Cleo," Zach Farley says, as we get out of the car. "I was wondering how you feel about my son."

I feel my cheeks go pink. That was pretty straightforward. "I've missed him. I care about him."

He nods thoughtfully. "I see that. But do you think you have any romantic feelings for him at all?"

This is getting very awkward.But I might as well tell someone what has been on my mind.

"I think that I might," I begin, cautiously, unsure how Daniel's father will take this. It's something I've only come to realize recently myself. "But the last time one of us had feelings like that, it ended badly. That was mostly my fault, and I don't know if he'll forgive me. Add to that, the fact that he doesn't believe anymore. I could never get involved with someone who doesn't."

He looks at me, understanding in his eyes. "I see. Please don't stop praying for him, Cleo. I'll be talking to God about him as well. I fear his disbelief has much to do with me not being a proper dad to him and...I hope he'll forgive me, too."

"I won't stop praying," I promise.

We're late enough already, so we hurry to the church building. We walk in and I leave Zach, who sends me a reassuring wink before he takes his seat, to find my family. They're near the front, sitting together on a pew. Mom and dad are holding hands as they stand and sing along with the entire church, Carpenter still looks half asleep but happy, and Eddie is casting glances at a pretty brunette girl a pew to the right. Oh, Ed. He's got a massive crush on that girl. Madeline, I think her name is. Emma stands next to Eddie, her body posture stiff. How come no one else notices other than me that she doesn't mean any of the words she's mouthing? I take my place next to her and start singing.

My mind wanders to Aiden while the sound of music and voices fill my ears. He still hasn't told Emma that he's been converted, that he's a Christian. I can't rush him and I know it's not my place to tell Emma, but I wish he would hurry up already, so that he can come to church without her been shocked at his appearance. I know it might take Emma a long time to get over it, but maybe it might convince her to turn back to God instead.

The hymn ends and we take our seats. As Pastor Hayes is reading out the announcements, the door at the back of the church rows creaks open. All heads swivel to see who it is, and my heart skips a beat when my eyes land on him.

Daniel.

He smiles just for me, looking into my eyes, before seating himself beside his clearly thrilled father. I turn my head back to Pastor Hayes. I try to concentrate on what he's talking about, but all I can think is what a joyous day this is. Zach is healed and it seems Daniel has had a change of heart.

Thank You, Lord, Thank You!

Author's note: Thank you for reading this. Please show some love by clicking that star icon and/or leaving a comment. Feedback is appreciated a lot.

I wanted to say something about miracles...it may seem unrealistic, what happened in this chapter. To humans, that sort of thing always will. But know that our God is a God of miracles, and that nothing is too hard for Him. I have heard of and even experienced that. So be encouraged.

By the way, as a side note, the...uh...interesting GIF is supposed to be Daniel. ;) (UPDATE: It doesn't seem to be working- does anyone know anything about why it won't?)

Have a lovely day, lovely person.

Chapter 28 - A Fool For Love

Before December 31st

AIDEN

"We're doing what?" I sputter, incredulously.

"Going back to Homestead for the December holidays," my dad says, almost amused at my outburst, his fork halfway to his mouth.

We're eating shepherd's pie, a favourite dish of mine, but I suddenly have no appetite. It must show up on my face, because mom frowns. "I thought you'd be excited, Aiden. You'll get to see all of your old friends again."

"Yeah," Stevie speaks up. "And I'll get to see that dreamy Jonathan again..." she fakes a swoon. Drama queen.

"That dude is no good for you," I snap, suddenly irritated. It's true, though. Jonathan is an immature boy who is already a player at the age of thirteen. I may have missed quite a few things when we moved, but him messing around with my sister was not one of them.

The thing is, I don't miss Homestead and the people there so much anymore. I don't want to leave my new home, or my new friends. I like Emma, I like Cleo, I like Crystie and Bryan. As well as Garth and Carpenter. Carpenter and I get on well, even if he's almost two years older than me, we agree on a lot of things and enjoy each other's company. And I've started reading the bible out loud to Garth recently, when we have time. His response has been very different to what I expected, and he wants to know more.

"What's wrong?" dad inquires, looking at me curiously. He, like mom, was most probably expecting me to be happy about this.

Well, nope, I'm not.

"You didn't tell me we were going to leave Stowe again so soon. What if I had made plans for the holidays?"

The truth is, even if I have been wanting to, I haven't made any plans. Mostly because I don't know what to do with myself about the issue of Emma. I love her. How can you hurt someone you love? I can't walk away and leave her, I don't know if she'll recover. At the same time, spending more and more time with her will only build our relationship up, and as the saying goes: the bigger they are, the harder they fall. It's a bit of a weird analogy, and one that Cleo came up with when she talked to me about it the other day, but she's right.

Waiting will cause more damage in the end, a nagging voice in the back of my mind tells me. I try to ignore it, and ignore the dangerous fact that I just haven't been able to make myself tell her I'm a Christian. It's okay, because I will. Eventually. But I feel I've been drifting further away from God because of it. I know I have to do it soon. If I get a chance to, I have to take that chance, before we leave for Homestead.

"Do you have plans?" Mom takes a sip of her water and puts down her knife and fork.

I shake my head and mumble something under my breath. My parents raise their eyebrows at each other, but say nothing about it.

"I know you'll miss Emma, sweetie, but it will only be for a short while," mom assures me.

"It's settled, then," dad announces. "We're going back to Florida as soon as school is out and we're staying until after Christmas."

Just when I was starting to enjoy the idea of a having a white Christmas, I think to myself, as I look outside the window at the snow that is falling down again. Not only do I have to leave the winter wonderland she loves, but I also have to leave Emma now. Not that I have any choice about that, whether I stay here or go to Homestead, anyway.

~ ~ ~

CLEO

Daniel comes to the service again the Sunday after his dad arrives in Stowe with the good news. After the sermon is over, everyone is chatting and pouring themselves tea or coffee. I search for Daniel in the crowd and when I spot him, I rush over to him. I don't even think about what I'm doing until I'm hugging him tightly, my face pressed against the warmth of his chest.

"I'm so glad you came," I whisper into his shirt.

"Hey now," he chuckles. "If I had known you were going to be so nice to me, I would have been coming here ages ago."

I sock him in the shoulder. "That isn't funny, Daniel."

He laughs again, but then becomes serious. "Cleo, I'm glad to be here, I really am. I want to thank you for praying for me and trying to get through to me this entire time. I can't describe how happy I am to have found my way back to Jesus again, and back to all of this," he spreads his arms, indicating the hum and friendliness of the people surrounding us, the community of people gathered together for one reason. Because we all love the One who first loved us. "I never want to leave again."

I look up at him, a big smile stretching my face. He isn't the same Daniel he was when we were kids. He isn't the same Daniel he was a week ago. He is a different person altogether, and I for one, like this new boy more than any other version I have seen of him. I study his face, unable to keep myself from staring. He really has nice features. His thick lashes brush his cheeks as he looks down and away from my gaze after a few beats, suddenly seeming to be self-conscious. I could kick myself for looking at him for too long. I glance away quickly, putting more space between us, and pretend to find an old man sipping his coffee particularly fascinating.

"I should probably go find my dad. If I know him, he forgot to have breakfast and is probably starving." Daniel says, trying to fix the awkwardness between us.

I nod. "How's your mom?"

A frown flickers across his brow for a moment before disappearing. "She 's...better."

"That's good," I tell him. "Well, I'll see you at school. And, next Sunday too."

"I look forward to it."

I turn to go, disappointed for some reason. Is it because I want to stay and chat with him? I'd prefer it if the answer were no, but something tells me it's yes, from the way my heart jerks inside of me when he reaches out to stop me from leaving by grabbing my arm. I turn around to face him again.

"Do you want to meet me at the Cactus Café later?" he asks, hopefully and somewhat breathlessly.

I feel a slow smile take over my lips. "I thought you'd never ask."

~ ~ ~

EMMA

Disappointment would be an understatement of what I feel when I hear that Aiden is going away for the December holidays. I know it will only be for four days, but I wanted to do something special with him. I didn't even have anything in particular in mind, I just wanted to celebrate our relationship. He has made my life so much fuller, I wanted him to know it. But that can wait until after Christmas, I suppose. Tonight, I'm going to focus on having a great time with Aiden at his sister's play. He picked me up at six and now we're on our way to the playhouse with Stevie in the back of Aiden's old jeep. The play starts at seven.

Aiden's mom was on some errand and is running late. She texted him to say she'll arrive separately. His dad is unable to make it because of work, which leaves just us three in the car. I don't know whether to be relieved because Stevie doesn't seem that upset about it or worried because it seems she's very used to it. Aiden has said that his dad is often very busy. Oh, well. It's not really for me to say or think anything about it.

Stevie is extremely nervous in the car ride to the playhouse. I come to this conclusion because of the endless, birdlike chatter emitting from her.

"Do you think I'll hurl when I see how many people there really are? What if I forget my lines? What if Mrs. Martin says I didn't do my hair right? What if everyone thinks that the Sugar Plum Fairy was the worst character in the entire play?" Stevie doesn't pause for us to have time to answer questions.

I stifle a giggle at her steady flow of questions. She's a talker, for sure. But she's also very sweet, and watching her chew her lip when I turn back to look at her reminds me so much of Cleo that I almost feel Stevie could be a second sister. "Stevie, you'll be fine. You're going to rock this thing," I assure her.

She grins at me, her hazel eyes sparkling. "You really think so?"

"Yes."

Aiden glances at me for a second. He isn't smiling, but his eyes are. He reaches out with his left hand to hold mine, his right still on the steering wheel as we drive straight. I don't know how I managed to find someone like him. I don't want to jinx it or anything, but I can't stop thinking that thought, over and over again.

~ ~ ~

The play is beautiful. The colours of the costumes and the scene setups are vibrant and captivating. Stevie plays her part so well that my hands sting from how hard I clap them when it's over.

"Did you see me, Aiden? Did you?" Stevie runs up to us in the dressing room we walk into after the show, makeup still coating her face, her purple tutu complimenting her skin tone and her blazing red hair caught up in a complicated style.

"Nah, I fell asleep before you even came on stage." Aiden covers his mouth, pretending to yawn.

Stevie frowns and pouts. "You did not."

He chuckles. "You got me. You were brilliant, Stevie."

She wraps her arms around him in a hug, before turning to me. "What did you think, Emma?"

"I think you did wonderfully," I reply, meaning it with all of me.

She beams at me, her coffee coloured orbs lighting up. "Thanks Em."

I smile inwardly. That's the first time she's called me Em.

On the way home, Stevie falls asleep. I was never able to fall asleep so easily at her age. But I suppose it could have something to do with the fact that twelve was the age Blaze changed my life for the worse. The nightmares would never leave me alone, and it often resulted in heavy bags underneath my eyes that made me feel ugly.

"What are you thinking about?" Aiden doesn't even look at me when he speaks.

Why does he always want to know? "The play," I lie.

He shakes his head. "That's not true. You've got that look on your face."

"What look?" I wonder out loud. "You aren't even looking at me."

He takes his eyes off the road for a second to stare me right in the eyes. "Yup, you've still got that look on your face. That look you get whenever you think about whatever you're thinking about."

I huff. "Ade, you're not really making sense."

"You know what I mean, though. Don't you?"

I turn my gaze to the window and don't answer.

"Is it Blaze?" he asks.

"Aiden..." I whisper. "Can we not?"

"Okay." He grabs my hand to grip it tightly like he did earlier, and his strength comforts me. "Emma, I've been wanting to tell you that I..."

His sentence fades away. "You what?"

"Never mind." He pulls his hand from mine and places it on the steering wheel. "Don't worry about it."

~ ~ ~

After December 31st

AIDEN

The night of Stevie's play was when I missed my chance, I guess. But I was thinking how cold my hand was when I took it from hers, and how she looked like an angel with her blonde hair framing her face in wisps as the streetlights from outside the car window filtered in and shone through it.

I was a coward. That's the most of it. Too afraid about what would happen if I told her the truth. Blaze had hurt her so badly before. How could I go and do something so similar?

But man, do I know now. I was foolish. I was a fool willingly, for Emma. And choosing to be foolish always comes at a price.

Chapter 29 - New Beginnings

Before December 31st

DANIEL

Cleo and I walk across the snowy park on a chilly Thursday, the day school ends, wrapped up in layers of winter wear and leaving footprints behind us. I smile at how much bigger mine are than her own tiny dents in the blanket of white.

"It's so nice to be with you again," she says, slipping her hand into mine and leaning against my shoulder.

My heart starts racing. I could try and tell myself that I was over Cleo the day she broke my heart, but it would be a laughable lie. I never stopped feeling this way for her.

I look down. She's using the hand that she hurt that night of the police station. I'm glad it's healed now.

"I feel the same way," I tell her.

She lifts her head and looks me in the eye. "Daniel, I..." she lets her sentence drift away in the cold air, and stops walking to face me fully.

"Yes?" I don't like how my hopes are shooting sky high, but recently I've been finding that it's better to hope some and be disappointed than to have no hope at all. Hope is a kind of fuel, it keeps us going.

"I wanted to say I'm sorry. For all I said a year ago," she eventually finishes.

I think back to that day I finally had the courage to tell her I liked her.

"Cleo!" I had been with her in this very park, and had been speaking very loudly to try and get her to concentrate on something other than the sketch she was drawing of me.

"Yes, Danny Niel." She'd always thought it was the funniest thing to put her two nicknames for me together. "Can't you see I'm trying to get your nose right?"

"I don't really care," I had said. "I have to tell you something."

She had heard me out. Cleo had always been a good listener. And afterwards she told me she could never return the feelings I had for her, that she only wanted to be friends. I remember scrunching up her half-finished drawing of me and throwing it down to the ground. I remember running all the way home.

And now here she stands, in front of me. Will she say the words I've been wanting to hear all this time?

Slowly, she retrieves something from her pocket. A piece of folded up paper. She hands it to me and I open it up. It's the drawing of me. She finished it and she kept it. It looks so much like me that I'm slightly taken aback.

"Cleo," I breathe. "You kept it?"

She nods. "I wanted to have it as a reminder of the boy...the boy that I love."

Did she just say love? "You mean, as a friend, right?"

She shakes her head, and then nods it again. "Well, yes. But more, too," she smiles at me shyly. "Daniel, I don't really know what I was thinking or how I felt back then. Not anymore. But I know what I feel now. And I'm sorry. For confusing you, for letting you down, for not being there when you needed me. That's why I brought you here, to the place where you spoke your heart. It's me doing that this time. I was wondering...could we start over?"

I look down at her, so many feelings swirling around inside of me that I can't think straight. Only one thought materializes. She has feelings for me. More than just the kind of feelings you have for a friend. I can see it in her intensely green eyes. My Cleo. That's what I want her to be. Mine.

"Yes," I say. "A thousand times yes."

I want to kiss her now. But she's young, and I'm young, and it might be too soon. It's okay, though, because I'm willing to wait. So instead I wrap her up in my arms, feeling the tickle of her warm breath on my neck, before lifting her up higher, so that she's dangling above me. She giggles as she looks down at me.

I having no intention of ever letting her go again.

~ ~ ~

EMMA

It feels so good to be home. Blaze is finally gone, and I can feel safe here once more.

Cleo sits on my bed as I unpack all of my clothes back into my closet. She's got a faraway look on her face and I smirk at her. I know who she's thinking about. The person who she went for a 'walk' with earlier today. "Wake up, Cleo. I don't like how Daniel has stolen all your attention."

She blushes. "Hey! That's not true."

I grin. "I'd appreciate it if you prove it by actually being here when you're here."

I don't know what I think about Daniel becoming a believer again. I had thought the guy was smart, but it turns out he went back to what he had wisely left behind. Christianity. Well, I won't be doing that. But I know it would break Cleo's poor heart if she knew, so I won't let her know. As long as I'm sure of my decision, no one else has to know. Other than Aiden, of course. He knows and he doesn't judge me. He left for Homestead today. I miss him so much already. But just thinking about him gives me a pleasant, tingling feeling. Emma Riley Harper...that has a ring to it, doesn't it?

"Now you're thinking about a certain someone," Cleo teases.

"Am not," I defend, my cheeks colouring.

"Are too," she retorts, her eyes twinkling.

"Fine." I roll my eyes. "Can I help it if Aiden is the most amazing boy I've ever met?"

Her eyes dull considerably. What's that about? But it's gone before I can say anything about it. "He is a really good guy," Cleo says, softly.

I leave my clothes to sit next to her. "Do you think he and I...will be together for a long time? Can you see that happening?" I ask.

She smiles, almost sadly. "I'm not the one who knows, Em. Only God knows."

Inside I'm scoffing, but I say nothing out loud. I know I'll love him forever, even if something were to happen to him, or to me. And forever is a long time. I don't need God to be in control of what happens in my life- I don't believe anyone can control that. I'll just love and live while I can.

"Only three more days until Christmas," Cleo speaks, startling me out of my thoughts. She gazes at the calendar on my wall.

"Yeah," I say. I glance out the window. The world outside is covered in white. "Want to go get some of Meg's famous choc chip cookies and milk?" I suggest.

"Definitely," Cleo says.

~ ~ ~

Meg, an elderly lady from church, runs a fundraiser for an orphanage each year in December. She makes all sorts of festive treats: hard, striped candies, plum cakes, mince pies, choc chip cookies and more. She sells them from her house and gives all of the money she makes to the orphanage. Every year, Cleo and I drop by to buy some cookies and put her flyers up all over town for her.

"Girls, girls, please come in," little old Meg ushers us inside with her walking cane. It has a piece of tinsel tied around it. "You are my best customers," she smiles a toothy grin, her cloudy blue eyes happy.

We walk into her kitchen. There's food everywhere. My eyes land on the heaped plate of delicious looking choc chip cookies. "Well, Meg, your cookies really do beat all else."

She brushes my compliment off with a flick of her hand. "Then you've not been out and about enough. My aunt Mandy used to make the most amazing baklava."

I laugh. "I don't even know what that is."

"I do," Cleo pipes up. "It's a Turkish dessert-"

"Yeah, we all know you're much smarter than me. You'll go to Yale and I'll probably be a college dropout," I cut her off, and wink at her to let her know I'm just joking. She shakes her head at me, smiling.

"Here you go, you two." Meg has put the cookies into a container and handed them to Cleo. Cleo pays and we both give the kind old lady a hug before we walk out the door.

We could have driven here, if Carpenter weren't out with his buddies. He took our only car, the white Nissan that we all call Snowball. I keep on telling my parents we should get another, since I can drive now. But money doesn't grow on trees, and I don't mind walking so much. Even if my boots do get soaked through because of the snow lying everywhere. Cleo and I head home in silence, posting Meg's flyers all over, on streetlight poles and walls and community dustbins as we go. She slings her arm around my shoulders when we're done, which is a little difficult for her, since she has mom's tiny build and I'm taller, like dad. She still manages.

"It's so lovely here. I won't ever get tired of having white Christmases," she breathes out heavily on purpose, and watches her breath leave in white puffs.

"So you think you'll stay in Stowe all your life?" I ask.

She shrugs. "I don't know. I'd like to."

We go quiet again, and the only sound is the noise of the snow crunching between our boots and the tar road.

Suddenly, all my breath leaves me in a whoosh when I feel two big hands grab me from behind.

Author's note: Well. There's a bit of a cliffhanger for you ;) Things couldn't go perfectly well, could they now? Anyways, that's chapter twenty-nine done and dusted...your thoughts and any votes are much appreciated!

We're coming near to the end of this book, actually. It's kind of sad. But I'm excited to finish what will be (drumroll) the second book I've ever completed! And I hope you have enjoyed it so far.

Here's to the next few chapters!

~Tane

Chapter 30 - An Old Enemy and an Old Friend

B efore December 31st

BLAZE

"Good to see you again." Roughly, I turn a bewildered Emma around to face me. I saw her and Cleo walking and just couldn't resist dropping by to catch up with her again.

She blinks. "Blaze? What- I thought, I mean, why are you still here?"

"What if I wanted to stick around, huh?"

Cleo tries to step between us. "Then that is none of our business and not something we want make our business," she says, trying to shove my arms off her sister.

"I didn't ask you, Queen Cleo." I swiftly grab her shoulder and pull her away, while still holding Emma with my right hand.

Cleo lifts her foot and then brings it down on mine, hard. Ouch. Didn't know the little thing could stomp so hard. But not hard enough to make me back off. I give her a hard push and she falls down onto the snow. I turn back to Emma. She still looks a little blank. She's gone silent and she seems to have turned into a statue, standing so stiffly that I'd be worried, if I cared.

"What's the matter, Em? You didn't expect this? Well, surprise."

Cleo is up again, suddenly, and she pulls something from her back pocket. A phone. "Blaze, if you don't walk away right now, I'm calling the police," she threatens.

"Cleopatra," I tut. "You don't want to get involved in this. Someone could get hurt." I move my hand to Emma's neck and tighten my grip so that she knows what I mean.

Cleo falters, as I expected. "I don't know what you want with Emma, Blaze. What you want with us. You already robbed her of so much."

I scowl at her. "I don't like it when people think they can forget about me and move on."

"She hasn't forgotten!" Cleo cries. "Do you really think she's forgotten?" She points at Emma's unmoving features, her blue eyes not leaving my face, her lips still not uttering a word.

I feel as if a rock has sunk to the bottom of my gut at her words, and I'm not sure why. Or maybe I am. What's the point of all this, really? What's the point of me harassing and tormenting this family? What's the point of my mom dying after a life of pain and suffering? What's the point of having a dad who has always hated me, no matter what I've done to try and change his mind? If there is a point in all of this, I don't see it. I can't find it. What do I have left? I had a mom who was too busy trying to survive to give me attention, even if I know she did care some for me, deep down inside. I have a dad who acts as if I'm not even alive anymore. Even when he did, he made my existence a living hell. I don't know which is worse.

And I have myself. But if there was something so wrong with me that dad made sure I never forgot it, then I can't be worth much. I can't be worth hanging onto. When I die, no one will write on my gravestone. No one will have anything to say about me. No one will remember who I was. Not that I'd blame them, because I don't even know who I am, not really.

But maybe they will remember me, if I take Emma with me.

Yes. This could work. I could have this, this one thing.

I have to know that none of them will forget me. I'll make sure of it. The Rayburns could never forget their daughter, their precious angel. And that boy I've seen hanging around town with her, I'm sure he won't. Therefore, they won't be able to discard me from their past, or even from their present, not like everyone else has, not if I can pull this off.

But I know now is not the time. I let go of Emma, and I walk a little distance back from her. Cleo rushes to her side to support her.

"Leave," Emma finally says something, her voice raspy. "Leave. Me. Alone." She pauses between each word and forces them out through gritted teeth.

I raise my palms. "I'm going. I'm going. You've got nothing left that interests me anyway," I direct my words at Emma, lying easily. Practice makes perfect.

Then, I walk away. But I'll be back.

~ ~ ~

AIDEN

We land at the airport in Homestead, Florida on a warm Thursday evening. Well, when I say warm, I mean warmer than Stowe. It never even comes close to snowing here. But if I hadn't been living in Stowe for the past three months, I would actually find the current temperature kind of chilly for this city.

"Huh." Stevie looks around, wrinkling her nose. "It's more boring here than I remember."

She could say that again. This place has nothing compared to the sights that Stowe boasts.

"Well, honey, I think it's just as grand as always. Look, how lovely the sunset is." Mom, ever the optimist, points in the direction where the sun looks like it's slipping away, off the edge of the world. Even it didn't want to stick around in Homestead for long, apparently.Stop being bleak, I tell myself, and just enjoy it while you're here.

But that's when I see her.

I could slap a hand to my forehead right now. I forgot. Of course they are picking us up from the airport. They're our friends. Our good friends, the people we were neighbours with for sixteen whole years.

Mikayla Brand and her family.

It's not that I don't like them. It's not that at all. In fact, they could be considered our second family. It's just that Mikayla has made it so apparent what she wants from me that it has made our friendship tricky. She has, after all, had an obvious crush on me since we were both eleven. I mean, I'm not normally able to pick things like that up very easily, but when I say it's obvious, I mean obvious. I know I have to be nice, though. She means no harm, and she's never wronged me. For a while before we moved, I kept on avoiding her, because kids at school had started joking around with me about her being my girlfriend. Which she wasn't, obviously. I just couldn't and can't bring myself to see her in that way. Sure, she's sweet. Sure, she's pretty. She has black hair, a pretty face and a bright demeanour. But she just isn't...

...Emma. I finished the thought, even though I really did try not to.

"Aiden! I missed you so much!" Mikayla throws herself into my arms for a hug.

"I...missed you too," I say, patting her back awkwardly and then pulling away.

"And I have so much to tell you." The wind pushes her dark hair into her face and she shoves it away again, before linking her arm in mine. "We can talk all the way home."

I don't like to admit that I cringed a bit at that. Thankfully, she didn't notice.

Mikayla and I have had some good times together, but I don't feel so comfortable around her anymore. One, she touches me when she doesn't need to. Maybe I should give an example. What I mean by that, is that we'll be chatting about something and then one of us will say something funny and she will laugh and, acting as if it's unconsciously even if it's not, she'll put her arm around my shoulder. Or, she'll hug a little longer than she needs to. Or, she'll lean her head against my chest at odd times. Or, she'll ruffle my hair and- well, you get the idea. Two, whenever my parents tease us about our possible 'future' together, I can't ignore how her face lights up or how she sneaks starry eyed looks at me. I honestly hope she's not counting on it.

But because she was my friend long before she started acting weird around me, I owe it to her to be friendly and a polite gentleman when I'm around her. Anything more would be impossible, because the image of Emma is always at the back of my mind.

In the car ride to the Brand household where we'll be staying, Mikayla makes good on her promise to talk. She tells me about how she redecorated her entire room, how her two little brothers are just as irritating as ever (according to her) and how she's taken to cycling.

"But how about you, Aiden? You've barely said anything. Tell me how it's been in Stowe," she commands me, after finishing a story of one of the pranks her brothers pulled on her recently.

"Aiden has a girlfriend," Stevie comments, before I have a chance to reply. She's beside Mikayla where she has been sitting, uncharacteristically silent, until now.

My face heats. Things are about to get awkward. Way to go, little sister.

Mikayla's brows furrow, and she looks at me as if thinking for a moment. There's no mistaking the hurt look in her eyes. But there's also confusion in there, as if this was definitely not something she was expecting. It tells me she was hoping for something else entirely. "Oh," she says, eventually.

We drive in silence for the rest of the journey, which isn't long. The Brands have two cars, so my parents are driving her brothers home in a separate car while Stevie, Mikayla and I are with her parents in the second car. I know her parents must have heard Stevie from the looks they keep on sharing. They aren't a good sign.

Oh, what a great way to start these four days away from home.

God, please give me strength and patience for this. Thank you that You promise to go with me wherever I go.

When we arrive at our destination, Mikayla gets out of the car without a word. I follow her out, but then realize I have to grab our suitcases from the trunk of the car and go inside of the house to put Stevie's in the room she'll be sharing with Mikayla and mine in one of the spare guestrooms. I'm going to have to talk to her about this, I know. Sooner or later. I'd prefer later, but procrastination is something I've been trying to fight.

My parents park in the driveway soon after we have, and the two boys, Derek and Dylan, waste no time rushing off to find Stevie so that they can play something together, probably a board game or something. The adults gather in the kitchen to talk over glasses of wine while a late dinner cooks on the stove, and I wander around trying to find where Mikayla went off to.

I eventually find her, sitting on top of the house's roof. We used to hang out there all of the time, and I don't know why I didn't think of it straight away.

"How did you get up here?" she asks me, kind of pointlessly since she must know if she managed to get herself up here as well, when I plunk myself down next to her.

"I used the ladder you used, genius. It was still where you left it." I keep my tone light. We've always been able to tease each other. But now, she stiffens at my retort. "I'm sorry, Mikayla," I tell her. "I didn't actually mean it. You know that, right?"

She nods, but refuses to look at me. And then, what I was afraid of happens. A tear forms in her eye and then quietly makes its way down her face.

"I'm sorry-" I begin, but she cuts me off.

"Don't worry about it." She wipes the tear away with her sleeve. "You don't have to say anything."

I open my mouth to try and explain myself again, but she simply shakes her head, and I get it. So I don't talk. Instead, we sit in the silence, underneath the now dark sky, until Stevie and the boys come to call us for dinner.

I have a feeling that's the last we'll talk about it. It's a good thing, because I won't be able to comfort her even though I don't like to see her sad.

I'm too busy wondering about Emma and if she's okay.

Chapter 31 - Christmas

Before December 31st

DANIEL

"Daniel, come on in, son," Mr. Rayburn welcomes me into the house. It smells like something is cooking, something good, and there are Christmas decorations haphazardly placed all over, just like the outside of the house.

I find myself smiling. Cleo's family always did go all out with the traditions and decorations at Christmastime.

When she invited me on behalf of her family and herself to their Christmas dinner, I had no reason to say no. And I didn't want to, anyway. Mom had woken up this morning and stayed conscious for just enough time to say merry Christmas and give me a gift, a new watch, before falling asleep again. She's exhausted, and I can't blame her. She barely gets any time off work. If she needs to spend the entire Christmas day sleeping, I understand. Dad had to get back to Boston to catch up on some work he left unfinished when he drove out here to see me. But he promised to be back again around New Year's. We discussed it together and both agreed that I should stay in Stowe until I graduate and then see where I go from there, instead of moving back to Boston where I've been expelled twice. So, having no one else to share this day with, I was both grateful and excited to join the Rayburns. I've missed her and her family so much.

And here she is now, dressed in the ugly sweater I gave to her for Christmas almost three years back when we were thirteen, which still fits her, with a big smile on her face. Her hair is loose, tumbling down her shoulders and back. I like it that way.

Something about how I feel right now reminds me of a quote from Dr Seuss' How the Grinch Stole Christmas, a movie we both loved when we were little.

"Then the Grinch thought of something he hadn't before! What if Christmas, he thought, doesn't come from a store. What if Christmas...perhaps...means a little bit more!"

"Hey, you." Cleo hugs me tightly.

"Hey, Patty." I return the hug, squeezing her. Her hair smells like vanilla and something else. Cinnamon?

"Daniel." She pulls away and narrows her eyes at me. "I suppose it won't be any use telling you not to call me that anymore, will it?"

"Nope," I say, popping the 'p' and brushing a strand of hair out of her face.

"Thought as much," she grumbles, but her eyes are sparkling as we walk into the living room where everyone else is.

After greeting everyone, I tell Cleo to wait for me inside while I talk to her dad. I have a question I need to ask him.

"What is it, Daniel?" Trent Rayburn asks me once we're outside in the cold on the front porch, for privacy.

"Sir, I think I can cut straight to the chase with you."

He nods, a knowing look in his eye as he watches me.

I take a breath and release it before talking again. "I also think you realize that I'm fond of Cleo. I respect your daughter very much. And, I think I love her as well."

His eyebrows raise. "I'm not surprised. She's a lovely girl, that daughter of mine. And you two have always been close. But the first thing I'm concerned about is, does she return those feelings for you?"

"Yes. She has told me. Not with words, but..."

He nods again. "I understand. But do you understand how young you both are?"

"Yes," I say. "I'm very aware of it. Which is why I wanted to ask you if I may date her, but only after we graduate from high school."

Mr. Rayburn makes me wait for his answer, as he strokes his chin and looks at me. Finally, he smiles at me. "Yes, you may, Daniel. I appreciate you approaching me first. You may, if Cleo says yes, and I have a feeling she will. You have my blessing."

~ ~ ~

EMMA

There are gifts underneath the tree, tinsel and paper star lanterns everywhere, the smell of cinnamon rolls baking in the oven, and laughter all around. Carpenter and Eddie are decorating cookies and making a nice big mess of it, too. Cleo and Daniel are starting up a fire in the fireplace and giggling over something together. Perhaps that's not the only fire they're starting. I smile at my own thoughts. Daniel is good for Cleo, I can tell. I think that everything they have been through, together and separately, has made them both stronger. Dad is helping mom cook in the kitchen, but personally I think it's just so that he can sneak kisses onto her cheek and give her spontaneous hugs. Everyone is happy, so I pretend to be happy.

But inside, I'm longing for Aiden.

I know I'm ungrateful. So many people don't have a family to call their own or somewhere to spend a cozy Christmas evening. I do, yet I still feel a little hollow on the inside.

It has to be Aiden's absence that's causing the emptiness.

Right?

I don't feel this way when I'm with him.

Or, it could be the recent incident with Blaze. If you can call it that, an incident. I have been having nightmares worse than ever now. They're longer, and more vivid, and scarier. I have this nagging feeling that Blaze isn't done with me yet, even though he said he was. I know better than to believe him. I keep on wishing Aiden were here, to comfort me. He wouldn't let anything happen to me.

"Emma," Cleo calls. The fire is started now, and young, weak flames lick at the wood piled up in the fireplace. "Come play a board game with us."

"Are we gonna play something?" Eddie drops his cookie on the tray and rushes over.

Soon, Carpenter, Daniel, Cleo, Eddie and I are caught up in a game of Cluedo. I suck at this game, but I'll do anything to take my mind off...

...Aiden.

Darn. I did it again, I thought about him.

"It's your turn," Daniel tells me, bringing me back to the present.

"Oh, right." I play my turn, without success.

In the end, Carpenter wins. The prize is a striped red and white candy cane, which I steal from him and then lick.

"Thief! Give back the honorary cane!" He tries to snatch it away from me, but I jump up and run away, sucking the candy cane as I go.

He chases me down and manages to take it back by tickling me until I'm weak. "S-s-stop," I plead, in between fits of laughter.

"Dinnertime, everyone!" Mom yells.

I recover from my tickle attack and we all waste no time in getting to the dining room. At the dinner table, with a huge meal laid out before us, we say grace before digging in.

"Daniel, it's so good to have you back," mom tells Daniel, who sits across from her, next to Cleo.

I can tell she doesn't only mean having him back in Stowe, but back in 'the body of believers' as she has always called it.

"It's good to be back," he grins, after swallowing a mouthful of roast potato. "And your cooking is just as delicious as ever."

Mom smiles at him, and I could be wrong, but I think I see a very faint blush, too. Daniel has always been a charmer. Well, before he went through that stage where he seemed to hate everyone and everything, ignored Cleo, and even got into a fight with Aiden...but he's so different now. I wouldn't say he's who he used to be. He's cheerful and kind, like the younger Daniel was, but he's also more mature now. And there's this light in his eyes that wasn't there a month back.

Because he's a Christian again? I can't stop myself from wondering.

But I quickly discard the idea, shaking my head to myself. No, that's a fairy-tale. That can't be it. I push the thought to the back of my mind and eat my food.

~ ~ ~

AIDEN

After a long but good day of taking a trip to the beach, which was quite a drive from where the Brands live, making a Christmas lunch together, eating it, then having tea and cake and opening presents, I'm finally just lying down on my bed, staring at the ceiling.

Mikayla's in my room, sitting on the floor, reading a book. I know she's tired too, because she isn't attempting to make conversation.

Well, until she suddenly puts her book down and gets up to sit on the only chair in the room. "Aiden, what are you thinking about?" she asks.

I turn onto my side to face her. "Well, I was thinking about how good dessert was earlier, but now I'm thinking about whether that will satisfy your question, and now I'm thinking that the answer is no, from the look on your face."

She quirks an eyebrow and shakes her head a little bit at me. "I think that's the most I've heard you say all day." Fiddling with the hem of her shirt, she looks down. "So, you weren't...thinking...about...her?"

She lifts her eyes to try and meet mine, but I look away. "I am now."

"Oh," is all she says.

"I thought you didn't want me to talk about it." I roll onto my back again.

"I don't, not really. But I'd like to know that my friend is in good hands."

I smile at that.

"What is she like?" Mikayla's back to scrunching and un-scrunching the bottom of her shirt with her hands, nervously.

"Well," I start. "She's kind and smart. And funny. And very strong."

She nods slowly.

"She loves her family and she loves nature and she has the prettiest blue eyes." After saying that, I realize I might have gone too far, so I sit up properly to see what Mikayla's reaction is.

But she seems calm. She gives me a shrug and a half-hearted smile. "She sounds great."

"She is," I agree. "But Mikayla, you are great too. You're going to find a guy who will make me seem pathetic in comparison. And let me tell you, he is going to be one lucky person."

She smiles properly now. "Thank you Aiden."

"It's true."

Silence.

"Thank you for being a good friend." I want her to know she has meant something to me, even if it's not as much as what Emma means to me.

Silence. And then, "Thank you, too."

I get off the bed and stretch. "Let's go see what my crazy sister and your mischievous brothers are up to now."

"Okay," she says.

Today is our last day in Homestead. Tomorrow, we go back to our new home. And I go back to Emma. I have a worrying notion in the back of my mind that something is wrong, and the sooner I get there, the better.

Chapter 32 - Not Enough Time

A day before December 31st

AIDEN

"Really, mom?"

"Really." Mom looks ready for anything. Well, anything except a warmer temperature. Clothed head to toe in a beanie, a scarf, gloves, earmuffs, boots and no doubt at least three pairs of socks, layers of shirts and a winter coat on top of it all, she looks like she put on her entire closet.

"But I was just about to go visit Emma," I say.

I haven't been able to see Emma once since I got home four days ago, even though that's all I want to do. Mom and dad have been insisting we spend some more 'family time' together, which has consisted of playing games such as Scrabble and Boggle, eating gingerbread cookies and drinking hot chocolate, skyping our grandparents who love to talk for ages (that must be where Stevie gets it from) and Stevie and I bickering with each other when we get bored. Now mom is insisting that we go for a walk in the absolutely freezing weather outside.

"Does she know that you're coming?" Mom asks.

I shake my head.

"Well, then, you can just drop by after our quick family walk." Mom smiles at me.

"But I want to-" I start.

"Enjoy a lovely walk with your sister and parents. I know." Mom finishes for me.

"You don't know-" I try again.

"How much you're looking forward to it." Mom grins at me childishly.

"Can we just-"

"Leave already? But of course," mom winks at me and then yells for my dad and Stevie to get here so that we can go.

I hang my head slightly in submission. I know when I've been beat.

Once we're out of the house and trudging, me miserably, Stevie with a skip in her step, and mom and dad amiably, across the sludgy, snowy lawn, I look up at the sky. It looks dark and threatening, like there will be a storm later.

"How long will this walk be, exactly?" I wonder aloud.

"Hmm...since you seem to be enjoying it so much, there's no rush," mom smiles smugly at me.

I give her a 'seriously?' look and carry on walking. Jiro, my German shepherd and faithful companion, bounds along beside us, chasing after Stevie.

We're walking on the pavement beside the street when an old black Ford whizzes past us. It gives Stevie a fright, which serves her right for walking so close to the road when I've repeatedly told her not to. It gives me a fright too, not because of the speed it passes us at, but because of the face I saw behind the wheel.

I thought he'd left, Emma said he had.

What is Blaze doing here?

~ ~ ~

After the hour long walk, we finally start to make our way back home.

"See, Aiden? That wasn't so bad, was it?"

"No," I tell my mom, before grumbling under my breath, "it was worse."

"I heard that," Stevie gives me a sly look.

"Me too," mom says, and throws a play punch to my shoulder. "You just wish it could be longer, don't you?"

I shake my head at her and grin. My mom can be a tease sometimes, and I'm grateful she has a sense of humour. My dad, on the other hand, is a very serious man. I glance at him now only to see he's frowning, oblivious to the moment the rest of us are sharing and probably deep in thought. Maybe he's thinking about something to do with work.

When we get home, I turn to mom with pleading eyes. "Can I go see Emma now?"

She smiles and pinches my cheek. "For the sake of young love, yes."

"Mom." I roll my eyes.

But I practically run to my car and hop into it. Next stop, Emma's house.

Upon arriving there, I see that Daniel is with Cleo on the front porch. They appear to be talking about something that makes them both laugh at the same time. A joke, maybe.

Cleo told me about Daniel and all that had happened. At first I didn't like the idea of them spending so much time together now, given the fact that the first impression I had of Daniel was of him bullying Cleo. But now, it seems that they are really enjoying each other's company. God's amazing plan played out and Daniel was saved, and perhaps that plan is even bigger than I would think possible, maybe it involves Cleo and Daniel having a future together. If that's going to be the case, then I'm happy for them.

That's the thing. God's plan is always more beautiful, more complex and more full of surprises than any of us could imagine.

But still, Daniel hasn't won my trust completely. Not yet. I'll be keeping an eye on him to make sure he doesn't cause Cleo any trouble.

"Hey," I greet them both, as I climb out of the car and make my way to the house.

Today is bittersweet. Mostly bitter, though. I'm both looking forward to and dreading this. Looking forward to it, because I missed Emma. Dreading it, because today is the day I must break things off with her.

I can't do this anymore.

It's not fair to her and it's not right for me to be keeping this up when I know we have different beliefs, different principles. I know that at the moment she thinks we both have the same views on Christianity. But she's in for a surprise, and she won't see it as a good surprise. I'm going to miss her and long for her like crazy, but the whole time I'm doing that I'll also be praying and trusting God to speak to her heart. I know that He has the ability to make everything work out for the two of us, to call her back to His arms.

"Hi, Aiden." Cleo waves at me. "How was the trip to Homestead?"

Daniel simply nods in my direction. His eyes say he's unsure about me, and I don't blame him, not after the fight we had. My bruises took quite a while to heal, his probably did as well. But maybe we can pretend that didn't happen.

"It was good, thanks," I answer Cleo. "How have you all been?"

"Good, all good," she smiles at me before sharing a second smile with Daniel, one that obviously means something.

"Is Emma home?" I ask her.

She shakes her head. "You missed her by about twenty minutes. She left for a hike by herself on Mount Mansfield, said she needed some time alone. Carpenter dropped her off."

"Oh." I frown, disappointed that she didn't invite me along. But I know what it feels like to need some time to think. "Well, thanks, Cleo. Do you think it's okay if I go meet her there?"

She shrugs. "Sure. She's been missing you, kept on telling me that she can't believe you haven't come by since you got home," she says this lightly to let me know that Emma is not really holding a grudge. Or, at least I hope that's the impression she's trying to give.

"I guess I'll just head on over there, then," I say.

"Good idea," Cleo agrees. "Just give me a call to let me know what time you two will be home. I don't want our parents worrying about either of you, since it looks like there will be a storm."

"What she really means," Daniel grins mischievously at her, "is that mother hen Cleo will be the one worrying."

"Hey!" She elbows him in the stomach.

"What?" He exclaims innocently. "You can't even deny it yourself."

She ignores him to look at me. "Bring her home to us, Aiden."

"I will." I give them a smile and a wink, before turning on my heel and heading for the car.

~ ~ ~

EMMA

I guess I just needed some time away from everything. To mull over facts. Facts like how Aiden hasn't even called since he got home, or that other fact that I actually don't want to mull over, the fact that I can't stop thinking about Blaze and his last appearance.

"You've got nothing left that interests me anyway."

His words echo in my head, haunting me.

That's what he said, but I've heard him lie so many times that by now I should be able to recognize his bluffs. The look in his eye when he said that to me scared me. Did he mean it? Or is he just biding his time?

I keep on expecting him to jump out of nowhere and yell 'surprise' or something, but it doesn't happen, and for that I'm grateful. It's just in my head. Actually, let me rephrase that. It's probably just in my head.

For now, it's only me, me and the mountain I've come to love ever since Aiden took me up here. I stand on the point where we stood when he asked me to be his girlfriend. The only difference is that it's covered in snow now. And, of course, Aiden isn't here with me. Staring out at the beautiful land that lies before me, I feel my heart thud in rhythm to the sound of the wind howling.

Whoosh, swoosh. Thud, thud. Swoosh, whoosh. Thud, thud.

"Well done, Em."

I jump at the sound of a voice behind me.

"I was going to plan a setup like this of some sorts, but you went and made it so easy without me having to lift a finger. Thank you," the voice says.

I don't even flinch. Instead, I think hard and I think fast. I need to buy myself some time. "I was right. You came," I say softly, and dully, like I'm bored. "You're so predictable."

"Am I now?" his voice is close to me all of a sudden, right behind me, his breath traveling down my neck. "Maybe to you. Only to you. No one else knows me well enough."

I gasp involuntarily when his hands clutch my waist.

"Scared?" he taunts.

I grit my teeth. "No. Not this time, Blaze. You know why? Because you're right, I know you well." I try to take a step away from him, and as I expected, he pulls me back, closer to his solid form.

I need to buy time, is all I can think.

"I know you well enough to not be surprised by you anymore. You may have thought me afraid all this time, but that was only because I never knew what to expect from you. You change personalities so quickly, so easily. But now, you've run out of the tricks you had stored up your sleeve. I've known you too long. You have nothing left to throw at me that I haven't already considered you're sick enough to do." I tell him all of this, hoping to provoke him and keep him talking instead of acting.

Because actions speak louder than words, and it's not pretty when he yells through his fists, or worse.

He growls a little at my words, before bringing his mouth down, close to my ear. "So you know exactly what I'm going to do to you?" he whispers, his voice both sharp and smooth as he leans in to me from behind me.

Even though my heart is pounding, I force out a pretence of a nonchalant sigh. "Oh, I don't really care anymore. But I'll guess, just to amuse you. Let's see..." His grip tightens at my not taking him seriously, and I almost let out a squeak as the pressure from his arms squeezes my ribs till it hurts. "Y-you're going t-to kill me," I stutter, as calmly as I can, stumbling over my words mostly because I'm still trying to breath as well as talk under the mercy of his constriction.

"Good guess," he murmurs against my hair. "It's so good to get you alone again. I've missed our time together. You're always so busy making eyes at that redhead."

I furrow my brows at this. He knows about Aiden. He must have been stalking me for a while. "Jealous?" I mutter.

"I don't need to be," he returns. "Because I know that you're mine. You've always been mine."

I stiffen. "No, I'm-"

But he doesn't allow me to finish, because he picks me up, bridal style yet not at all romantically, making me stop midsentence. I can see his face now, his dark brown eyes and lips set in a twisted smile.

"Put me down," I breathe, his face so close to mine that I barely remember to. But not in a good way, not the way Aiden makes me forget to breathe. This is different.

"Sorry, I kind of don't want to." He grins a cruel grin. "Because you and I have somewhere we've got to go. Together."

I frown at him. He looks away, and I follow his gaze. He's looking down, off the edge of the peak of the mountain that we stand on.

And it's then that I know what he's thinking.

"Ready?" he asks me. He knows that I know.

I start kicking, clawing at him, yelling, screaming. It's no use. There's no one out here to hear me but us. He holds onto me until I go limp, like a ragdoll in his arms. "Why?" I ask, breathlessly. "Why?"

"Because." He states, simply. "Like I said, you're mine, and I'd like to keep it that way."

Then he starts walking closer and closer to the edge. I fight back again for a little while, but he grabs my wrists with one of his hands and holds them together in a death grip that makes me cringe in pain, while he secures the rest of me with his other arm. The wind whips at my face and hair and I look above to see that the sky looks stormy and angry. I always wanted to die on a pretty day, not an unkind, unfeeling day like this.

You don't always get what you want, do you?

I close my eyes and wait for him to jump, because I know he will. I know him, and I know he will do this thing that most others wouldn't even consider doing, killing another life along with his own. What did I ever do for him to want this for me? His body tenses and his knees bend as he prepares himself to leap off the mountain, with me in his cold, hard embrace.

Well, I tried. I tried and I managed to buy myself a little bit of time.

Just not enough time.

Chapter 33 - Snowstorm

A day before December 31st

AIDEN

I whistle as I drive to Mount Mansfield, even though my mood is anything but happy. Whistling a tune off the top of my head is just something to do to try and keep my mind off what I'm going to have to tell Emma.

The journey is a pretty one, snow starting to fall all around me as I park the car and get out. It's bustling at the bottom of the mountain. Apparently, everyone- well, mostly tourists, want to visit it while it's still covered in thick snow. I don't blame them, it's quite a sight to see. Especially for one who has not seen much of the white, icy cold substance in their life. Like me.

I'm confident I'll find Emma where we went together the last time I was here. No one often goes there, or so Emma told me. There are too many that are afraid of heights, the same as myself, I suppose. It's a secluded peak on the mountain overlooking a frightening drop. I wonder how many times she's been there without me, alone, and if she thinks about me when she goes there.

I take my time walking to the small office where I can buy a ticket for a cable car ride up, and even when I do get there, I have to queue in a long line. I could take my car and drive up the winding roads on the mountain, or even hike the trails, but I'm too worried that Emma will have come down by the time I get there. The cable car is the fastest way up, and I don't want to miss her.

"Did a blonde girl buy a ticket from you earlier?" I ask the lanky, bored looking man in the office, who wears a raincoat with the hood pulled over a cap.

"Nah," he gives his nose a rub, his bland expression not changing. But then he pauses, his hand falling away from his face. "But…I did see a blonde lass, just one girl, take a trail up on foot. No one else is crazy enough to do that in this weather, so I thought to myself, what does she think she's doing?"

It sounds like Emma to me. "Thanks," I say.

I pay for my ticket and soon I'm in the cable car, on my way up, surrounded by a crowd of people. They wear bright colours that are harsh on my eyes after the peaceful, toned down landscape around me. A few, the tourists most probably, talk different languages as they babble over the height we're climbing, slowly but surely. All of them speak loudly.

I hear a crackle from a speaker of some sort, and then a voice sounds out.

"Ladies and gentlemen, this will be the last ride of the day. It looks like there's a storm heading this way, so please don't be long on Mount Mansfield. Enjoy the view, but keep in mind that the last cable car leaves in less than an hour once you arrive at the top."

I don't have much time to find Emma, then. Hopefully it will be easy and she will be where I think she is. I close my eyes and try to think about her, and not about how high up I'm going to be.

Don't open your eyes, Aiden. Don't look down. Whatever you do, just don't-

I open my eyes and look down. Immediately my stomach lurches and I start to sweat.

Idiot.

Oh, the things I'm willing to do for her.

~ ~ ~

CLEO

I told Aiden to call me to tell me what time he and Emma would be back. He messaged me instead. He sent it to me not very long after he left to go find her. They should be back before seven pm, he said, and if not, then it's safe to say we should worry.

I look up at the unfriendly sky. There's a monster of a storm on the way.

The problem is, I'm already worrying. I have this queasy, unsettling feeling in the bottom of my stomach about today. About Emma, about Aiden. It's been awhile since there was a snowstorm in Stowe, and there haven't been any seriously damaging ones in any case. I tell myself this, trying to calm myself down. But it doesn't work.

There's something else, something more that is tickling my nerves.

Then it comes to me. Blaze.

He isn't, or well, wasn't supposed to be in town anymore. What if he hasn't left, even now? What if he is looking for Emma and finds her before Aiden does?

Daniel, who sits beside me, takes my hand and rubs it. "What's wrong, Cleo?"

I shake my head. But Daniel cocks his own at me and lifts a brow. I know I can't hide the truth from him. "The other day..." I start, but falter. He squeezes my hand in encouragement. "The other day, Blaze talked to Emma and I."

Daniel frowns. "I thought he had left town?"

"We thought so, too. But he hadn't. And now, I'm thinking...what if he still hasn't?"

It's not much of an explanation, but when he looks at me, I know he understands. "C'mon," he says, pulling me up by the hand. "I think we should go."

"Go where?" I ask.

"I think we should make sure they're both okay."

I know he's talking about Emma and Aiden. I nod, because I agree. Because I love my sister and I can't let anything else happen to her.

~ ~ ~

DANIEL

I give my helmet to Cleo. It's dangerous to be driving without one on my own head, but I'd far rather she have the protection.

"No," she says, handing it back to me. "You must wear it."

"I want you to," I tell her, firmly. "Put it on."

She thrusts her hands onto her hips and gives me a look. "Please," I add.

Probably because she knows here and now is not the right time, she drops the argument and pulls the helmet on, securing it to her head.

"Let's go."

I saw the worry in her eyes when she talked to me about Blaze and just knew that we had to go. Even if it's only to comfort her, even if we find out that it was simply a hunch.

We have to go after them, because I've learned that hunches are more trustworthy than you'd think.

But despite trying to convince my head and heart that it will all be okay, there's an awful cloud hanging over us, like something bad is going to happen. I don't mean an actual storm cloud, although there are a few of those too, but there's something else as well.

Please, Lord, protect us all. Bring us all back safely.

I can't explain this sense of foreboding that I feel, but I can't ignore it, either.

Cleo gets on the motorbike behind me, and wraps her arms tightly around my waist. There isn't a moment to stop and think how warm and nice her arms feel in that position.

Now is the time to drive, and drive hard.

I start up the bike and the engine lets out a few small growls before roaring to life. I rev and we speed away from the house. Snow has begun to fall, again. I think this is the snowiest I have seen Stowe in my entire life. All December it's been snowing, on and off. Normally I would like it, but right now it's only annoying. It lands on both Cleo and I, wetting us through our clothes to our skin. And it looks like the sky has a lot more to offer us. Just wait, it seems to be saying, with the ugly looking clouds gathering together like bruises blemishing the horizon and the rumbles sounding out. You haven't seen anything yet.

~ ~ ~

EMMA

I will try and fight Blaze one last time. Even if I end up dying while I try. As he braces himself to launch, I stretch my leg upwards and kick him the hardest I can, in his face. He grunts and steps back a bit, but doesn't let go of me. I swing my foot at his head again, and this time, he drops me into the snow. Through the snow, I can feel the hard ground, and my body already aches from the impact of my fall. But I can't worry about that now. I have to get up.

I have to run.

I pick myself up off the snow blanketed earth and force my stiff, cold limbs forward. But I'm not fast enough, and all too soon Blaze stops holding his nose to walk in front of me, blocking my way. I smash into him at the pace that I had been running, which wasn't very fast. Did I think I would get away, really? He shoves me back a small distance and then hits me across the face with the back of his hand. It's so fast and so hard that I fall again, my face stinging and throbbing at the same time as I lie flat on my back.

"You're pathetic," he says. His tone is calm and cool, but I know he is furious. "Just accept that you can't save yourself and that there's no one here to save you." He gives an odd shrug, and looks down at me with some sort of sick sympathy in his eyes.

Then he smiles an ugly smile.

Anger rushes through me, filling me. I will not go easily. This is the last time he raises a hand against me, the last time he says something like that to me.

When he reaches down to pick me up, I bite his hand. He gives a yell of pain, but doesn't give up. This time, when he grabs me, he wraps his hands around my neck and picks me up from there. I panic as the ability to breathe leaves me. His hands are strong, too strong. He adds more pressure to my neck, slowly cutting off my air supply. I bring up my own hands to try and pull his off, but I don't have to, because he stops, suddenly, putting me down gently and removing his hands, as if he hadn't just been strangling me. I feel weak from suffocating, and when I almost stumble into a faint, he catches me, swinging me up into his arms once again.

I give up. My breaths are coming in shallow gasps as I gulp the air greedily. But my body feels small, tired, frail. I lie still in Blaze's hold, and even though I fight against it, my head lolls against his chest of its own accord.

Maybe I should just go to sleep. It could be peaceful, and I wouldn't have to be awake to feel myself leave this world with the one person I've hated for so long. My eyelids drop slowly as he takes step after step, nearing the edge of the drop.

Sleep. So peaceful. Such a nice way to forget about everything, to not remember. To not think. I long for it to come, and it will, I know, because my breathing and my heartbeat are slowing now.

But then it doesn't. As Blaze jumps, I can't stop my eyes from flying open, the same way I can't stop how we seem to be flying through the air. No, not flying. Falling.

A shiver runs down my spine as the moment slows down, almost stopping completely. It's like everything is in slow motion, even my thoughts. Aiden's face flashes through my mind, and I smile. I remember him covered in sweat and his hair all mussed up as he carried me when I hurt my ankle. Cleo's face is there, also. I remember her arm on my shoulder as we walked through the snow, two sisters that would always be just that: sisters. Companions.

Suddenly, when I think that gravity's powers will be what ends me, its force changes when I feel a sharp yank as both Blaze and I are pulled back by something. By someone. Blaze wasn't expecting this and his arms loosen around me until they're gone, and I'm the one falling, slipping away slowly. He is the one who lands safely, and I am the one sliding off the edge, as I try to hold on. But there's nothing to hold onto but wet snow that only seems too eager to slide away beneath my body.

Before I can scream, a hand reaches out and grabs me by my arm.

Aiden.

Oh, I missed you, I think.

He pulls my up in one big tug, grabbing my other arm as he takes me away from the edge.

I am not falling. I am safe from dropping off this cliff to my death, because of Aiden. But the image of Blaze's contorted face behind Aiden tells me that neither of us are completely safe yet. Blaze trips Aiden up from behind and attempts to plunge into him with his fists from above, but Aiden rolls away and jumps up, ready to fight back.

And then the snow starts to come down in earnest, fluttering around us in hectic flurries. I watch as Aiden and Blaze wrestle each other in the whiteness, the world booming and the earth's roof crackling with the warning of the dangerous snowstorm that is descending upon us.

Author's note: Sooo...what did you think? Be brutally honest with me. And know that you are awesome for having read this far and that I appreciate any comments or votes you have given me, very much. xxx

Have a fabulous day/morning/afternoon/evening.

Chapter 34 - Rescue

A day before December 31st

AIDEN

When I find Blaze with Emma, I don't have time to think things through. My brain simply makes the connection and I see red when I realize what he's doing. I won't let him. Over my dead body if anything.

I run forward to grab his hood and pull back with everything I've got, and catching him unawares, I manage to force him to the ground. But he no longer has her in his arms. Then I see that she is about to disappear off the edge, as the snow slides away, taking her with.

"Emma!" I shout. I don't know if she can hear me through the snow and wind, but that doesn't matter.

I haul myself forward and just as she's about to slip off, I catch her. Suddenly, I feel Blaze's hands on me from behind. He's trying to push us both off now. I lift my leg and thrust it back, donkey style. Satisfied with the noise that comes from him when my foot hits his stomach, I finish dragging Emma to safety.

All of a sudden my feet are kicked out from beneath me and I land on my chest, my breath leaving me in a rush. I try to think past the dizzy aching of my head. I'm vulnerable on the ground, I need to move. I roll onto my back and launch myself up. Blaze is ready for me. This is the first time I've seen him properly, up close and in person. He's built solidly, with large biceps and meaty fists. He's tall, and his eyes are dark. This is the part where I'd like to say that I can take him down easily, but...he's almost twice my size in width. And I don't mean he's fat. When he comes for me, lunging forward, I know he'll be able to knock me down. I decide I'll just face him head on. I won't be a coward. Then I feel a hand on my ankle. It takes me a moment to realize it's Emma. She pulls on my leg so that I fall to the side, and we both watch, on the ground, as Blaze passes by us, his face changing from menacing to frightened as he realizes his mistake.

It's too late for him to slow down in time and he falls off the peak, without a sound.

Emma gasps, and my heart stops beating for a moment. I may have felt something near to hate for Blaze, but I didn't intend for anyone to die. "I didn't mean to," she whispers. "I didn't really mean for him to fall."

I turn to her on my side, still heaving from having the air knocked out of me. "Emma, it's not your fault. You were trying to help me."

But she's shaking, tears dripping off her chin. I reach out to cup her cheek and feel that she's ice cold. "Emma, listen to me. We're going to get off this mountain now. The storm is only getting worse."

She shakes her head. "I killed him, didn't I?"

"No," I sit and pull her up as well by her trembling shoulders. "No, Emma. Listen to me. It's going to be okay. I promise it will be okay."

Her eyes look glazed over and a tear has frozen on the tip of her nose. I use my thumb to brush it off. Then I stand and walk over to where Blaze fell.

I have to see for myself if he's really gone. What I see relieves me: a small ledge, not very big but big enough, juts out from the mountain, and Blaze's body lies sprawled upon it. He might still be alive.

Please, God, let him be alive. I don't want Emma to have to live with this.

"Emma, we have to go now. We need to go and get help. I saw Blaze on a ledge, he might still be alive." I speak quickly and urgently. Emma looks up at me. When she doesn't move to get up, I crouch beside her. "Are you hurt?"

I run my eyes over her face, noticing for the first time the big, ugly bruise on the right side of her face.

"No. I'm fine." She says, snapping out of her trance and getting up. I get up with her.

I pull off my jacket and put it around her. I put my arm on her shoulders, keeping her close to warm her, and we start making our way blindly through the storm. I don't know where I'm going and it's too difficult to see through the swirling snow. Panic rises in me. But for one of the first times in my life, I know I'm not alone. There is Someone who knows my every thought, my ever fear, my every feeling.

Jesus, show us the way.

We keep going. I put one foot in front of the other, again and again. I plead with God to lead me in the right direction.

And then I see it. The road that will lead to the bottom of this mountain .Thank you, Lord.

Emma huddles against me, her teeth chattering. I know she's cold and in shock, but we have to get down from here. "Emma?"

She looks up and meets my eyes. "You have pretty eyes. So blue, like the swimming pool in the summer," she says, dreamily.

Is she delusional? Is she getting hypothermia? I don't know, but I hope against hope that she will be okay. "Can you run with me? The faster we get down, the better."

She nods. "I'm pretty fast," she murmurs.

I smile at her despite the situation. "If you get tired, tell me."

She nods again, and then we pull apart so that we can both run. I'm glad she's not so confused that she doesn't know what's going on- she seems to know what to do. We both follow the road, my wet shoes squelching and squeaking each time they hit the ground. Running with her reminds me of when we went for a picnic on Spruce Peak and we chased each other.

We've been pounding the ground with our weary feet for maybe another ten minutes when I hear a sound. The sound of an engine.

What...? I wonder. A motorcycle?

Unsure if I'm making things up with my mind, I don't believe it until I start to make out two faces appearing, through the blurry, snowy haze. Daniel and Cleo, sitting on a Harley-Davidson.

They slow down as they reach us, and Cleo jumps off the seat, pulling the helmet off her head and rushing over to Emma. "What happened?" She directs the question at me, because Emma seems to be out of it again, staring into the distance instead of talking to or looking at anyone of us.

"I'll tell you everything later," I say. "Right now we need to get her out of the cold."

Daniel also gets off the bike, kicking its stand in place and coming over to us. "Cleo, do you remember when I let you drive the Harley the other day?"

"Yes."

"I need to you drive it down this mountain now, with Emma. Can you do that?" he asks.

It makes sense. They both need to get back to Stowe as soon as possible and away from this snowstorm. And Daniel and I can run on foot.

"I can," Cleo looks unsure, but willing. "Come on, Em."

She helps a wordless Emma onto the bike and puts the helmet on her head.

"Cleo." Daniel walks over to her. "Be safe, okay?"

"I will," she promises.

I look at Emma. "Emma, I need you to call for help as soon as you get to the bottom, okay?"

She'll know what to do. She doesn't reply, but her eyes tell me she will.

Then they're both gone, a droning sound disappearing into the darkening world. Daniel and I look at each other. We have no choice but to work together now. Besides, I already admire him for his quick thinking.

"Blaze is back there. I don't know if he's alive, but we need to get a rescue helicopter out there." I tell him.

"Okay," he says. "I run track at school, so...shall we?" He gestures to the road ahead of us.

I smile. "We shall. Last one to the bottom of this wretched mountain is a rotten egg."

We run through the bitter weather without stopping.

~ ~ ~

CLEO

The snow and wind lifts and flies through my hair, chilling me. But I feel alive as I drive Daniel's motorbike down Mount Mansfield, Emma holding on from behind. Alive and grateful that she is alive.

Jesus! You are so good! You are always watching over us. Thank you for warning me, thank you for Daniel who listened to me. Please be with him and Aiden, give them strength and protect them from getting hurt.

I haven't heard Emma say a word since Daniel and I found her and Aiden. Even when we get to the bottom, she doesn't say anything. I try talking to her, but she refuses to reply, or is just too cold to. We rush to the office, and I thank God it's not closed. The man who sits in it is drinking something steaming from a mug and eating a donut. When he sees us he almost chokes. He then quickly opens the door and leans out.

"Come in, you two crazy girls!" he yells at us.

Well, I don't have to be asked twice. We almost fell off the bike when I parked it, we're so stiff and frozen. We stumble into the small but cozy building through the door that he opens wide for us, before he shuts it hastily. There's a fire crackling in a fireplace and we both near it, holding out our hands to the warmth.

"Aren't you supposed to be closed for the day?" I wonder, as I look out the window at the raging storm.

He shrugs. "Didn't feel like going home. Now, what on God's green earth were you two doing out there?"

I open my mouth to speak, but Emma beats me to it. "You need to call the search and rescue team. There's a man up there who might still be alive, somewhere below the west peak that barely anyone ever visits."

Wow. She still has a voice. I'm glad.

The man doesn't waste any time, and I'm glad for it. After he listens to her, he almost trips over himself as he fumbles for the telephone. He dials a number and blabbers a bunch of words into it that I don't pay attention to, because I'm watching Emma. She looks almost blue with cold, there's a nasty, large bruise stretched across her right cheekbone and her hair is wet and stringy.

"You okay?" I ask her.

She smiles at me. It's a mistake, because her lips are so dry that the bottom one cracks open and blood trickles out. She winces, but doesn't give up smiling. "I will be."

Author's note: Hey people. I'll be real with you- I don't like this chapter, and I'm unsure of how well it turned out. Maybe you can help me fix it by pointing out things that don't flow nicely or any mistakes you see. Otherwise, a vote is much appreciated. ♥

Also, I know the photo is not exactly perfectly fitting for this chapter, but I liked it, so...yeah.

Hope you have a lovely day/morning/evening/afternoon/night, wherever you are.

Chapter 35, Part 1 - Love Your Enemies

Half an hour before December 31st

EMMA

I stand in the doorway of the hospital ward, a blanket wrapped around me and Aiden by my side. I rest my head against his shoulder as we both take in the image of an unconscious Blaze on the starch white hospital bed.

"I shouldn't be," I whisper, "but I'm glad he lived."

"Me too," Aiden replies. "I think he would have had more power over you if he had died."

I think I understand what he's saying. If Blaze had died tonight, his death would have haunted me forever, worse than the memories I already carry around with me.

My parents and Cleo and Daniel are waiting for us in Doctor Roberts' office. I don't know why, but I felt I had to see Blaze like this. Asleep and weak. Maybe because I wanted some sort of satisfaction in seeing that he finally knows how it feels to be unable to defend oneself. But now that I'm here, watching the steady rise and fall of his chest and his sunken, pallid face, I don't feel satisfied. I just feel sad. He will never walk again; Doctor Roberts had told us. And I don't feel triumphant about it at all, as I would have expected to just a few days ago.

I shake my head slightly at myself. My eyes wander to the clock on the hospital room's wall. It reads half past eleven, pm.

"We should go," I tell Aiden.

He doesn't talk, just slings an arm around my shoulder and leads me to the doctor's office. I thought leaving Blaze and the smell of the ward he was in would mean leaving the sorrow I feel, but I find I was wrong.

Don't cry, I will myself. You're just tired, that's all.

Aiden opens the door to the office and we walk in. Immediately everyone stands up. Dad walks over to us and envelopes me in a hug, whispering something I can't quite hear into my hair. Mom looks ready to cry, and I know why. They were the ones who insisted that we be hospitable to Blaze, that we forgive him. That I forgive him. But they don't have to feel guilt, I don't blame them one bit. I blame their religion. They wouldn't have let him near me if they hadn't been brainwashed into 'loving their enemies' by the bible.

Love your enemies. Who ever heard of such a stupid idea? Just look where it gets you.

Behind my parents, Cleo and Daniel stand side by side, and I smile across dad's shoulders at them. They would make a lovely couple. Maybe one day...

"I'm so glad you're safe." Mom joins the hug.

"Me too," Aiden speaks from behind me.

Me three, I think.

"We should get home," dad says.

"Yeah. I think everyone is exhausted," Aiden agrees.

I turn to him and give him a smile. "Thank you. For everything." I hug him with all the energy I have left.

"Anytime, blondie," he murmurs to me, his breath warm on my neck and his arms strong around me.

We say our goodbyes to each other and the doctor before splitting up. Daniel drives his bike and Aiden takes his car.

The trip back home is silent, but not in a bad way. Everyone is tired. Cleo and I sit in the back, and my parents are in the front. Halfway there, Cleo falls asleep, leaning against me. I rest my head on her own dark haired one and soon welcome the dark oblivion of sleep as well.

~ ~ ~

December 31st

"I don't know, Aiden," mom looks at me, biting her lip in worry. "She's still recovering. It's only been a night, after all."

"Mom, I can decide for myself, you know." I let out a dramatic sigh.

Aiden arrived at our door at two in the afternoon. I was the one to open the door and the softness I had seen in his eyes when I looked up at him made me feel I would melt. But along with the tenderness I saw in his face, there was something else. Regret? Fear? Sadness? Or a mix of all three of those? I don't know, but I have to find out. When he asked me to go for a walk with him, I had grabbed my coat and was on my way out- then mom found us. Now here she stands, putting up a stubborn fight. She's a lot like Cleo. Or maybe I should say Cleo is a lot like her.

"Mom, I'm fine," I insist. "The worst damage that has been done is this." I point to the bruise on my face, indicating what I mean.

"And I need to talk to Emma about something, if it's alright, Mrs. Ray- I mean, Marlene." Aiden smiles sweetly at my mom.

Aha, so he does have something on his mind.

Mom relents. "Okay, just a walk. And it can't be a very long one, alright?"

Aiden and I both nod.

I shrug on my coat and link my arm with his as we walk out the door. Home isn't very far from the very centre of Stowe, so it doesn't take us long to be amongst the stores and cafes and little bookshops. We stroll away from the house and further into town along the pavements, watching busy people get on with their busy lives. Aiden doesn't speak for a long time, but he whistles now and then. I wonder when he's going to say what he wants to say. I hang on his arm, matching my pace with his. We stop to cross the street, following our noses to the wonderful smell of the bakery on the opposite side. Once we're inside, I order a glazed lemon poppy seed doughnut and Aiden orders a cinnamon bun.

We sit at the table in the bakery, eating our food contentedly. But halfway through my doughnut, the silence finally gets to me. "Aiden, what was that about needing to talk to me?"

Ideas flash through my mind. A promise ring, maybe. Asking me to the New Year school dance, perhaps. Talking to me about what happened yesterday, could be.

Aiden swallows before he answers. "Um, yeah, that. Emma, I need tell you this very bluntly. Is it okay if I...give it to you straight, no sugar coating?"

This doesn't sound good. But I want him to always be able to tell me everything, and I'm not one to want any sugar coating, so I nod.

"Emma." His blue eyes glint with seriousness as he puts down his bun. "I want you to know that I am a Christian."

I blink at him. And then I laugh. I laugh and laugh and take another bite of my doughnut to stop myself from making a scene with my laughter.

He looks at me, concern filling his face. "It's not a joke," he says, solemnly.

His brows are furrowed and his mouth is pulled tight. I realize he means it. And I almost choke on the mouthful of doughnut I was chewing.

Author's note: Sorry for the short update. You'll just have to hang on till the next part of this chapter. :) In the meanwhile, please comment, vote, and all that jazz.

And thank you for reading!

Chapter 35, Part 2 - December 31st

December 31st

AIDEN

I watch as all Emma's previous mirth leaves her face. Her skin turns a little pale, and she starts coughing on doughnut. I'm up immediately, patting her back.

"Are you okay?" I ask.

She shakes her head, tears streaming down her cheeks from her choking fit. But she manages to swallow, and I sit back down. She wipes at the tears on her face.

I have been praying about this since last night when I hugged her goodbye. As much as I desperately didn't want to, I knew it was time. I had to tell her.

Lord, give both of us wisdom. Please may she listen to me.

"Emma," I begin, ready to tell her what she needs to know. "It's amazing. You have to believe me. My life is completely different. I am changed. I have joy, I have a Father who loves me, I have a friend in Jesus. Being a Christian is not what you thought it was. It isn't going to church or praying or being perfect, it's having a relationship with our Saviour. And Em, He loves you. So much."

She doesn't respond. Her baby blue eyes look at me in disbelief. They're so light and clear, unlike my own slightly duller blue. How I love those eyes. I never thought they would watch me in that way, like I'm some sort of monster.

"Emma?" I reach out for her hand, but she pulls it away. "Please say something?"

She grinds her jaw and drops her doughnut into its box. "You want me to say something, Aiden? Well, I'm sorry if betrayal is the sort of thing that makes me close in on myself." She stands up, placing her palms on the table and leaning forward slightly. Her voice lowers. "I thought it would be something I could handle because I've been through it before with Blaze, but I didn't think things through. You see, I thought I could take this kind of thing from anyone I couldn't trust. Easy. So I made sure I only trusted a few people. It's less dangerous that way, Aiden. Things like this don't happen." The mask of anger slips from Emma's face for a moment and I see the pain beneath it. "Obviously, I made a mistake in trusting myself to choose who I can trust."

She takes a breath after that. We both stare at each other, and the emotions running wild between the two of us are almost tangible. Then she turns to leave. I can't let her leave. I love her too much.

I love her?

Yes. I'm only realizing it properly for the first time now, but I love her.

"Wait, Emma." I grab her arm.

"No!" she snaps, yanking it away. "You're no better than Blaze, you know that? No better!"

My heart breaks at those words. The hurt I feel when I can see it in her face, that she means it, is almost too much to bear. I see other feelings playing across her features as well. Incredulity, confusion, mistrust, fear even. My gut wrenches at the realization of the last one.

Fear.

She doesn't know if she can believe me about anything else now. That much is obvious. But she has to know I would never hurt her physically, and as long as I live I'll do my best to not hurt her like this again. If she would just listen...

"Emma, I promise it's true."

She scowls at me. "What's true? Are you even capable of telling the truth?"

I wince at her tone. "Christianity is not what you thought it was."

She shakes her head slowly. Tears slip unchecked down her face. Her voice shudders and goes soft with her next stab to my heart. "No, Aiden. You are not what I thought you were."

I stand up to walk over to her. If I can just make her stay, talk this out with her, maybe I'll have a chance of fixing this.

Please, Jesus, give me the words to say. I don't have them. Speak to her heart, for me.

"Stop!" Emma shrieks. "Don't come a step nearer."

I freeze in place.

"Just don't. I'm leaving now, and you may not follow me."

She turns and runs out the entrance of the bakery, covering her face with her hands. I watch from inside as she stops beneath a streetlight, her shoulders shaking, the afternoon light dancing across the waves of her blonde hair. I can't take it anymore. I go to her, leaving our table and half-finished food behind. Standing behind Emma as she sobs, I touch her shoulder. She jumps and turns to face me.

"Aiden, go away."

A sick feeling plummets through me and lands at the bottom of my stomach at the cold dismissal in her eyes.

Emma. I love you. Please believe me.

I open my mouth to speak, but then she runs. She just runs. Across the street. Without looking left, or right.

Without waiting for the car that slams into her body before she gets to the other side.

Chapter 36 - The Colour Red

December 31st

EMMA

"Emma!"

It sounds like it was supposed to be a scream, but the sound of someone calling my name is already fading away, so I can't be sure. It doesn't matter, anyway. All that matters is...what matters? I try desperately to remember what I know matters. The world is moving around me, yet I can't hear anything anymore. But I can feel. I feel that whatever I'm lying on is hard and uncomfortable. I wish I were lying on my bed instead, that would be nice. Because I feel kind of sleepy. And I'm wet. Why am I wet? I lift my hand. It's covered in red. Red. Such a pretty colour. Vibrant, full of life, blazing. It's dangerous, and also beautiful. But it means something else as well. What does the colour red mean again? I don't know. I can't remember. What is that disgusting taste in my mouth? I attempt to get rid of it by spitting, but the taste doesn't leave.

Oh, well. The vile taste won't matter once I'm in dreamland. I might not be on the most comfortable bed, but it will have to do, because my body feels exhausted.

But then a face comes into view. I know that face, that dark copper hair, those deep blue eyes, the strong chin. Aiden.

His mouth moves, but no sound comes out. Does he know that I'm sorry? I hope he does. I hope he knows that I'm sorry for what I said to him, for running away from him. I hope he knows that he's nothing like Blaze. I was wrong. There's something else I hope he knows as well. Should I tell him? I think I would if I could, but I can't speak, try as I might. My mouth feels like it's full of cement. My head feels weighted to the ground. And it feels like a hundred knives have been thrust into my side. Why? What happened?

Aiden kneels next to me. "Emma."

I feel a surge of excitement. I heard him! But I'm confused, because it looks like he's shouting and yet his voice sounds like a whisper to me.

"Emma, Emma, please stay awake."

Anything, anything for you.

I fight to keep my eyes open. It's difficult because it's like my eyelids have suddenly become too heavy to lift. Maybe all of me has turned into cement.

That's sad. It would be horrible to never be able to move again. I start crying at the thought, surprised that I still can. Tears trickle down my face, cooling my cheeks. Come to think of it, all of me has started feeling cold now.

My eyes connect with the image of someone standing next to Aiden. A stranger, a man with a beard. I've never seen him before. He's holding a phone to his ear, a look of panic on his face as he talks into it. Aiden is holding my hand now. I can't feel it anymore, but I can see that he's grasping it. I feel all funny on the inside, like I'm melting. Maybe I'll just be a pool of red in the end. That wouldn't be so bad. Red is a pretty colour, after all. I try to smile at Aiden. Why does he look worried? He shouldn't be. I'm fine. Just fine.

This isn't the first time I've thought this, but I love how Aiden's hand fits into mine. So many pictures roll through my mind now, almost like a slideshow is playing. Aiden carrying me. Aiden laughing at something I said. Aiden looking down from the hot air balloon with me. Aiden's fingers entwined with my own. Aiden kissing me in the snow. Other memories come to me as well. Memories of my family, and of Crystie. Having a picnic with them. Smiling at mom, teasing dad. Playing baseball with the boys. Ruffling Eddie's hair, punching Carpenter in the shoulder. Sharing my secrets with Cleo. Dancing around the room with Crystie in a red dress.

Aiden. He promised me he'd take me for a ride in a balloon again. He promised. That's why I know I'll be okay. Because he wouldn't lie to me. I'll be okay and we'll be together again, in all the ways I want to be with him. Finishing high school together, getting married, having kids. I blush, or at least I think I do, at the thought.

Before all of that can happen, though, I need to take a nap. I can't keep my eyes open anymore. There's just one thing I need to tell Aiden and then I can sleep.

"I think..." I try so hard to get the words out, but it feels like I'm slowly drifting away.

Wait. I'm going to tell him. I'm ready to tell him.

"Emma?" Aiden looks so upset. I wish I could tell him he doesn't need to be unhappy. "Emma, stay with me. What do you think? What?"

"I think...I think I love you," I tell him.

And then the darkness closes in on me, swallowing me. I don't mind. He knows now. He knows.

~ ~ ~

AIDEN

"You can't do this to me." I whisper hoarsely against her neck, as I bend over her, lifting her into my arms. "You can't come into my life and make me feel the way you do and then leave. I won't let you. Do you hear me? I said I WON'T let you!"

But her head lolls away from me, her eyes closed and the parts of her face that aren't covered in blood so pale she could be a ghost. I touch my fingers to the pulse on her delicate, white throat to check if it's still there. It is. Oh, thank God, it is.

The man who was driving the blasted car crouches beside me. "The ambulance is on its way, son," he says, his voice sombre. "I'm so sorry about this."

Everything in me wants to turn to the man and yell at him, to beat him to a pulp. To shake him and throttle him. To scream in his face about how he's cruel and sick to have done this to my Emma. Yet I know it isn't his fault. Emma crossed the street at the wrong time.

So instead, I bite out, "Thank you."

I swallow, trying not to cry here and now. Maybe if I stay strong, Emma will be able to take from that strength. Maybe if I hold her close enough, so that we are almost one, I can breathe for her and she won't have to worry about breathing for herself. Maybe, as I clutch her broken, wrecked and bleeding body to my own whole one, she will heal.

I can tell myself all of this, and still, nothing will stop me from knowing the truth. Maybes are no good.

But I can pray.

Jesus! Save her! Please. She doesn't know You, yet. She hasn't accepted you. Don't let her leave the world like this!

I allow my eyes to wander from her face down her body. My stomach turns at what I see. Her right arm lies squashed against her side in a strange position, covered in blood, and the tip of a bone sticks out of her skin where her once perfect collarbone was. I lift up her coat and then shirt, my hands shaking as I do. Her side looks like a galaxy of blooming bruises, covering her ribs in odd, mottled colours. There's a mashed in dent in her ribcage amongst the bruises that looks like an unnatural dip into her waist.

I resist the urge to let out a strangled cry. How fast was the stupid car going?

Then I hear it. The sound of the ambulance's siren is like music to my ears.

It happens so fast that I don't even have time to speak. People jump out of the ambulance van and I help them put Emma into it. They tell me to stay behind, but I won't, and I win, earning a spot next to her as we drive to the hospital. They rush about around me, putting an oxygen mask on Emma's face, saying something about how she's struggling to breath, something about internal bleeding, stripping her shirt to assess the damage, asking me if I'm okay, asking for Emma's parents' numbers.

It's all a haze, because I feel lost as I watch Emma's still form and only one thought materializes.

I was the one who upset her, I was the reason she ran outside the bakery. I was the one she was running from. Me.

I did this.

~ ~ ~

Emma lies on the hospital bed, her skin so anaemic and colourless that it would almost blend into the crisp white bedcovers if it weren't for her golden hair and the bruises all over her.

It hurts me to see her so damaged. And it's my fault.

But there's something more important than that right now. Something that isn't physical or material, rather, something spiritual that hasn't been resolved yet. She doesn't know the One who changed my life and hasn't accepted Him as her saviour. And I don't know if she will live long enough to do that, or if she'll even want to. She hasn't wanted to believe in Jesus for a long time now, why would she want to today?

Please, Lord. Just wake her up, even if it's just for a little while. I need to talk to her about You. Don't let her die this way. I'm begging You. I want her to go home to You. Please do this for me. I may not be able to love her and have her by my side for the rest of our lives in this world the way I want to, but please will You save her soul for all eternity.

I pray to God with the same plea I've been begging Him with for the past hour.

You say it Yourself in Your word, Lord-

"The Lord is not slack concerning His promise, as some count slackness, but is longsuffering toward us, not willing that any should perish but that all should come to repentance."

Two Peter chapter three verse nine. Jesus, I'm hoping against hope. It seems stupid to the rest of the world, but I'm hoping.

The doctor's words ring in my ears as I'm praying. "I don't think she'll make it to see tomorrow. I'm sorry." I want them to go away, but they won't.

"Internal bleeding, trauma to the head, it will be a miracle if she even lives a few more hours…"

The said fate taunts me. Will I never get to hear her laugh again? That lovely laugh of hers. I miss it already.

I look at Cleo, who stands next to me, her lips moving silently. I know she's praying as well. When she meets my eyes I see that hers are filled with fear. Her hands are trembling, so I take one in my own and squeeze it. She tries to give me a smile of thanks, but I can tell she's going to cry.

Emma's family are all here in the room. Carpenter and Eddie stand side by side, their faces so similar in the way that they are both shocked and distraught. Her parents stand next to Cleo. Mrs. Rayburn is sobbing into her husband's chest and Mr. Rayburn looks broken himself.

The door opens and Daniel walks in. Cleo must have called him. Behind him, the doctor enters as well. Dropping my hand, Cleo rushes into Daniel's open hug. Daniel nods at me and everyone else, his eyes full of an unspoken apology as his arms wrap around Cleo, before they leave the room together. I know he'll take care of her, I've seen for myself how close they are now.

"May I talk to you in my office, please, Mr. and Mrs. Rayburn?" The doctor asks, the very picture of cool and calm. I wonder how many times he's had to deal with shaken people like us.

They walk out after Daniel and Cleo, Emma's mom still crying. The boys follow, Carpenter saying, "I can't see her like this anymore."

I can't help but feel they're giving me some sort of privacy with Emma, even though they are her family. And I'm grateful as I'm left alone in the room, staring at Emma.

Please…wake her up. Even if it's just long enough for me to-

A small moan emits from Emma, cutting off my prayer. Her lashes flatter and she opens her mouth, widening her eyes fully. I am by her side in an instant, taking the hand that is not broken.

Thank you, Lord. Thank you.

I know that God will give me the words I need to say. And I will tell her something I've wanted to tell her the moment I saw her twisted and bleeding body lying on the tar, and even more so after her own confession.

"I love you too," I whisper.

Chapter 37 - Going Home

December 31st

EMMA

I blink at Aiden as my vision clears from completely distorted to slightly more sharp, a bit confused for a moment. He loves me? He's never told me that before. Then everything comes rushing back to me. The anger. Running away. Crossing the street, but not making it in time before...

The car. I was hit by a car. That must explain why I feel so strange, why it's so hard to breathe. And I told Aiden I loved him. Now he's saying that he feels the same. Which might also contribute to the fact that I'm struggling to breathe.

I have a pounding headache and when I try to move, I yelp. Aiden's face and the room around me are both slightly fuzzy, like I'm watching a blurry video. Everything hurts. Everything except for my right arm, which I can't feel. Something tells me this is not something I'm going to recover from.

"Ade?" my voice comes out in a broken waver.

"Yeah?"

He comes nearer and when his face is closer to my own, I'm able to see that he's watching me with grief and angst in his eyes. That can only mean one thing. "Am I going to live?"

He swallows, his Adam's apple bobbing up and down. "I..."

"Don't lie to me," I whisper. "You haven't so far, so don't start now."

He looks away, his eyes glassy. "I don't know, Emma. I really don't know. The doctor said that..."

"That I'm going to die?" I croak.

He turns to face me again, and nods. Bravery. It's a trait of his.

"Huh," I murmur. That's all I can say.

What do you say to something like that?

Then a cough takes a hold of me, wracking my whole body. With each cough my chest feels like it's going to collapse into itself and the rest of me, especially my abdomen, aches so sharply with pain that I wouldn't be surprised if someone told me I had swallowed a bunch of daggers. I cough and cough until blood comes up. Aiden grabs a tissue from the table next to me and wipes it off my chin, gently.

I don't want to ask what's wrong with me. I don't really want to know. Most probably a lot of long medical words that I'll struggle to pronounce. And it won't help me accept that I'm going to die, anyways.

"Thanks for telling me the truth," I say, once the blood is all wiped away.

He gives a half-hearted grin. "Sure. No sugar coating, right?"

I smile weakly as well. "Right."

He looks like he wants to say something, but he must be struggling to get the words straight. His lip is trembling and he runs his hand through his hair over and over again. I don't blame him, I don't know what I would say if this situation were the other way around.

"I'm sorry," I tell him.

He pauses with his hand midway through his hair. "For what?"

"For everything." Another small hiccup-like cough escapes me and I fight to compose myself so that I can finish. "For saying you're like him. You're nothing like him."

He bends over me and reaches out to stroke my cheek with the back of his knuckles. "I'm sorry I didn't tell you sooner."

Oh. Right. He's a Christian. I didn't forget, but I was hoping it wouldn't be brought up again. I have no energy left to be angry with him, though. I love him. I just want things to be right between us before I go wherever I'm going when I die. Maybe I'll just enter a state of nothingness. Maybe it will be bliss. But now that I'm so close to it, I realize I'm scared. What if heaven and hell are both real? What if God is real, and I've spent the last four years running from Him?

"It's okay," I finally say. It takes a lot, almost everything I have left to speak now. Probably because I'm busy dying.

"Emma." Aiden's hands are playing with my hair now. He rubs it between his fingers as he looks down at me. "It's not. It won't be okay until I can convince you that you're mistaken."

It may seem a harsh thing to say to a dying person, but I can sense that what he's telling me now, he's only telling me because he cares for me. I don't answer. The thing is, I don't even mind if he tries to convince me this time. Perhaps I'm ready to give in.

"Do you still believe what I say to you? Do you still trust me, despite everything?" he asks.

I think about that for a moment, but I don't actually need to mull it over at all. It's already been set in my mind for a while now, it hasn't been shaken out of place. I trust him. I know I do.

I nod yes, and even that is an effort.

"Then," he removes his hands from my hair to finger my chin. "you'll believe me when I say that Jesus Christ isn't a myth, a fairy tale, a child's story. He's for real."

He's for real.

I'm baffled at the feelings churning within me. I'm wondering for the first time in a while. I'm doubting myself. Since when have I doubted my cynicism towards Christianity? Since when have I been one to buy this stuff or second guess about this? The answer comes to me, creeping into me slowly and silently almost like it's tip toeing, afraid I'll send it right out again.

Since you're about to die.

I never doubted my decision before because I didn't have to. I woke up and went to sleep without things changing, every day, every night. Nothing to fear. Nothing happened to me the night after I decided I was no longer a Christian, so I thought I was right. I thought I could live without Him.

But what happens if I die without Him?

There's nothing I can guarantee myself this time. Nobody has told me what death is like, or what waits for us on the other side. Nobody has promised me that I will be okay.

Or maybe Someone has.

A verse that I tried to bury deep beneath piles of other words from movies and books and people comes to me. I attempted to hide it away from myself, but it's always been there. Maybe it has been waiting for just such a time as this.

Romans chapter ten verse nine. "If you confess with your mouth the Lord Jesus and believe in your heart that God has raised Him from the dead, you will be saved."

I lick my cracked lips. I'm running out of time to decide what I truly want. Do I want to be safe? Will I be safe if I believe this? I look at Aiden, running my tongue over my dry lips again. His eyes are pleading with me. And then I make my mind up. If he believes this and lives with this kind of faith, then that's good enough for me. I can see it in his eyes, like something, or someone familiar and warm is calling to me.

I know Who it is.

I believe in You, Lord. I believe in You again. I believe that You rose from the dead. I believe that You have the power to save me. Whether I live or I die.

An almost overwhelming peace settles into my heart. I made the right decision this time. I want to tell Aiden about the choice I've made. I want to see my family again, and tell them as well. Tell them everything. I want to hug all of them. There are so many things I still want to do. But that isn't for me to control.

I try to smile at Aiden. It's difficult, because it's like half the feeling in my groaning body is gone already, which is actually a relief. The pain is fading. But I fight to give him one last smile anyway. Maybe he'll understand. Maybe he won't. Hopefully he'll remember my last words. It's okay. Because they're true. I want him to know that. I could worry about him, about what's going to happen to him now, but I know there will be Someone to take care of Him.

As for me?

I'm going home.

~ ~ ~

AIDEN

Her eyes close, the thick dark blonde lashes coming to a rest against her pale cheeks. Her lips are formed in a hint of a smile even as the beeps on the heart monitor join into one long blare and screech into my ears. Death is an ugly sound.

This isn't fair. I didn't even get to hear her say 'I love you' again. I don't know if her soul is saved. I don't know what her family will say when they find out that she woke up and I didn't call them before it was too late, before she was gone.

She is gone.

The reality of it hits me at full speed. I wonder if this feels similar to being hit by a car, like Emma was.

Except I'm not going to die because of it, of course. I'm going to live. But I'm going to have to live without her. Without her. Suddenly, I feel it can't be true. She'll wake up just now, she's just sleeping. She'll give me that teasing grin and she'll call me Ade again. Of course she isn't dead. Why would she be dead now, after everything? After all we've been through and all we've come to mean to each other?

She can't just go and die on me now.

"Emma!" I yell. "Wake up. Wake up. I want to talk to you again. Talk with you the way we always do, the way I've never been able to talk to anyone else. There are so many things I want to do with you, things I don't want to do with anyone else. Please wake up."

But she lies still. Her chest doesn't rise. Her face is slowly turning whiter than it already was. The heart monitor is screaming at me. She's truly dead. Truly gone. A lone tear trails down my cheek.

Why, God?

Is this really how her life is supposed to end? I don't even know if she knows her Lord, Jesus Christ.

Take heart. She is Mine.

The words almost seem to be audible. But I don't understand them. Is God telling me that she's with Him now? I'm not completely sure. No, I'm far from sure. But I have to believe that. It's the only thing that's going to help me survive this.

Tell her I'll see her again.

Because I will, and I look forward to it. There are some loves death cannot defeat. Not our love. Not the love she had for her sisters and her brothers, for her parents. And not the love of the God who is greater and stronger than this. Stronger than anything else there will be to face.

I will face it all when it comes. Right now, I'll allow myself to crumble. I am human. A sixteen-year-old boy going on seventeen. Human.

As I kneel besides Emma's bed, sobs that I can't hold back anymore escaping me, I think to myself that I wasn't ready for this. I wasn't ready to lose her in this way. All that I'm holding onto now is that I don't have to rely on myself to get through this.

When we are weak, He is strong.

Epilogue

After December 31st

CLEO

I think God gave Daniel to me as a gift.

In the blur that followed Emma's leaving this world, he was always there. Hugging me. Murmuring words of comfort to me. Holding my hand. Talking to me even when I refused to respond.

I had lost a sister, and the scar it had left was ugly. But in that same year I gained someone who meant a great deal to me. Normally grief pulls people apart and sets up walls between them. I'm glad normal doesn't always happen. Instead of leaving me when I was angry with everyone and sorrowful about everything, Daniel stayed. He stuck with me. He was the one who noticed when I didn't want to eat and forced me to. He was the one who called me every night just to make sure I was okay. He was the one who took me to the park and told me to draw, months after Emma died.

It was on a sunny summer Sunday afternoon that I finally knew I'd be fine. Daniel took me to the place where I'd laid my heart bare to him. He handed me my drawing pad, something I hadn't touched in a long time.

"Draw." He ordered.

"Draw what?" I asked. I didn't want to draw. I hadn't drawn since December the thirty first and I didn't plan to anytime soon.

It was like I felt that if Emma was dead, the beautiful, kind Emma that I had loved, then the drawing that I had used to love as well could die too. For all I cared.

"Draw a squirrel, a leaf. I don't know, Cleo. It's your magic, not mine. You have a way of looking at the world and then managing to capture the beauty that is there using just a pencil and some paper," he told me.

I looked at him for a long time. Eventually I threw my drawing pad away from me and sat down on the grass, folding my arms like a little kid. He fetched it and came to sit opposite me. He placed it in front of me, then pulled away one of my hands to splay it against his own, like the scene from Tarzan where Jane and Tarzan sit on a tree together.

Then I realized. It was true, it was real that Emma was never coming back. But Daniel was here, right in front of me, breathing, golden skin glowing, green eyes piercing, his hand pressed against my own. He was real too. And this was the reality I wanted to focus on. So I picked up my pencil and I sketched.

I haven't stopped since.

"I knew you had it in you," Daniel had grinned at me.

I smiled at him. "Thank you for finding it for me."

He'd looked away, almost as if he was shy. "It was worth it. Just to see that look in your eyes again. I missed that sparkle."

Later that day, on the way home, we kissed. It was an innocent, quick kiss. But it was full of promise.

~ ~ ~

AIDEN

Emma's family wasn't mad at me for having those last few moments with Emma, as I had thought they would be. They were just sad. So bitterly sad that it made me even sadder than I already was.

Cleo stopped speaking for a few days. She wouldn't say a word to anyone and her eyes were always red from crying. But the day after the funeral, she finally spoke again. She was sitting with Daniel, Carpenter and I on the Rayburns' front porch. It was silent, until, suddenly, she just started listing all the things she knew Emma had loved. Summer, mountain air, blueberry muffins, Meg's cookies, whoever Meg is, giving Eddie frights, play wrestling Carpenter, teasing Cleo, singing along to country music, something Emma had never told me she liked, dressing up, swimming. She talked about how Emma hated white chocolate, and told us that she had secretly owned a Barnie mug. Then both Carpenter and Daniel joined in as well. Carpenter mentioned how she used to come to his room when she got scared at night when she was a little girl. Daniel said that he couldn't quite forget the one time at the age of nine, when he dropped his ice cream and she gave him hers.

Little did they know, but they were giving me treasure. I did my best to carefully remember every little thing about Emma Riley Rayburn. I tucked away the small and big memories of all shapes and sizes, and every little quirk of hers, every expression that her face had made, into safe hiding places in my mind.

I still take them out and look at them, sometimes. It hurts, but at the same time it comforts. And there's no way I'm letting them go.

I stayed in touch with her family. More than that, actually. They never once made me feel unwelcome in their home, even though in my eyes, I was the cause of Emma's death. Still, her parents loved me as if I was their own son and I loved their children as my own siblings. Carpenter gave great advice. Cleo cared. Eddie was optimistic. They were lights in my world and still are. Only a year apart, Stevie and Eddie became really close as they both grew older. Eddie would tell her stories from the bible and eventually she wanted to start coming to church with me, making me rejoice inwardly.

One afternoon, on a particularly bad day, when I was having flashbacks and couldn't stop thinking about Emma when she looked so sickly and feeble in the hospital bed where she died, Stevie knocked on the door of my room.

"Come in," I said.

Stevie tip toed in, watching me with those big hazel eyes as she neared my bed where I was sitting. "Have you been crying?" she asked.

I sighed and nodded. She pulled her lips in a funny way and looked at me strangely. "But it's a happy day."

I looked at her, confused. "How so?"

"Because, Aiden," she said. "I want to be baptized."

I had smiled so big that I almost forgot how awful I had felt a minute ago. Almost.

That same day, we were both baptized. I felt as if I were clean afterwards. New. Different. And I was nearly certain that if Emma had been here, she would have been happy for me.

I was okay for a while.

Then Daniel and Cleo got engaged, later on in their lives. I was so glad for them. I took them out for dinner to celebrate. I'd come to care for them both so much, and seeing how happy they were together was great. I told them I saw it coming a mile away, making them laugh. I told them that I hoped that it was the start of an amazing journey. I told them that Emma would have been over the moon. I didn't tell them that I screamed into my pillow that night, full of frustration and envy and disappointment. I didn't tell them that while I was looking forward to seeing their future play out beautifully, it also reminded me of what Emma and I could have had. What we could have been.

It was better they didn't know.

And life went on. My parents were sympathetic, but they had always thought that what Emma and I had was not going to last anyway. Because we were young, and young love dies fast, right?

But ours didn't. Even after she was gone.

I prayed all the time, asking for peace. I cried, sometimes. I threw myself into my studies towards the end of high school and then even more so when I was in college, trying to forget. I wasn't trying to forget Emma or who she was, but rather other things. I fought for high grades through the gloom that came after her death. I could get lost, spending hours doing math. I knew I was good at math.

But I was even better at making mistakes.

And that was what I spent in the time after that December day trying to forget- the mistakes I had made. The 'if only' haunted me. Perhaps, I'd think to myself, and I still do now, perhaps if I had just told her sooner, she would have lived. Maybe she would have changed her mind about her atheism. Maybe we would have gone to college together, got married, been a family. But I've said it before. Maybes are maybes, they are not something worth dwelling on. Yet, I still haven't learned that. Maybe it takes time.

On my nineteenth birthday, I remembered my promise. How had I forgotten for so long? I don't know. But I was grateful I remembered, so that I could keep it. I asked Emma's parents for her ashes, which they hadn't buried, but kept in a smallish, engraved box. They didn't even ask questions when they gave it to me, and their trust in me after everything that had happened made me even more emotional than I already was.

I drove to an old friend's house and asked her if I could borrow her hot air balloon. She said yes. And as the balloon lifted me into the sky, it seemed that it was decades ago that I took Emma up with me. Both of us excited and a little thrilled by the slight sense of danger that comes with being so high above everything else, me feeling a little dizzy and sick because of my height phobia. Two sixteen-year olds without an idea of what lay ahead. I'd made a promise that day. I'd promised her it wouldn't be the last time we did that together.

Now here I was, making sure it was a promise kept. When I was floating above a thick, green forest, I opened the lid of the box and let her ashes fly away. Then I was done- I had done what I'd said I'd do.

And in letting her go I found a way to keep her close forever. It's not something I could explain, even if I tried.

The pain, the guilt, the regret. The longing. Hints of it still follow me wherever I go. But I will find freedom. This season will pass and another, happier season will come. I know this because I trust my God, and He has a plan.

A very good plan.

The End

www.ingramcontent.com/pod-product-compliance
Lightning Source LLC
Chambersburg PA
CBHW071955070526
44583CB00015B/1201